DIVINE MOMENTS FOR WOMEN

Everyday Inspiration from God's Word

DIVINE MOMENTS

MOMENTS

for

WOMEN

Everyday Inspiration

from God's Word

Tyndale House Publishers, Inc.

Carol Stream, Illinois

Visit Tyndale's exciting Web site at www.tyndale.com

TYNDALE, New Living Translation, NLT, and the New Living Translation logo are registered trademarks of Tyndale House Publishers, Inc.

Divine Moments for Women: Everyday Inspiration from God's Word

Managing editors: Ronald A. Beers and Amy E. Mason

Contributing writers: V. Gilbert Beers, Rebecca J. Beers, Brian R. Coffey, Jonathan Farrar, Jeffrey Frasier, Jonathan Gray, Shawn A. Harrison, Sandy Hull, Rhonda K. O'Brien, Douglas J. Rumford, Linda Taylor

Designed by Julie Chen

Edited by Susan Taylor

ISBN-13: 978-1-4143-1226-2

ISBN-10: 1-4143-1226-1

Printed in the United States of America

14   13   12   11   10

7   6   5   4

Introduction

The goal of *Divine Moments for Women* is to help you experience a breakthrough with God, to show you how and where God is at work to get your attention each day. If the Bible is really a blueprint for living, then God, through his Word, should be able to respond to any question you have for him. And he is! As you read the questions and portions of Scripture in this book, you will discover how God's answers to your daily needs are clear and help you to see with "spiritual eyes" how he is trying to break through to you. Sometimes God seems so big and mysterious that you may wonder whether he would truly bother with you. But he loves you and is trying to get your attention every day. This little book can help you notice the divine moments when he is trying to show you how much he cares. You can read straight through this book if you like. You can also use it topically when you are looking for God's help in a certain area or to gain more clarity about what God says concerning something particularly important to you. We pray that this little book will be meaningful to you and will help you experience many divine moments with God.

—The editors

Abilities

How can I make the most of my abilities?

A Moment *with* God

[The Lord] takes no pleasure in the strength of a horse or in human might.

PSALM 147:10

It is not by force nor by strength, but by my Spirit, says the LORD of Heaven's Armies.

ZECHARIAH 4:6

It is not that we think we are qualified to do anything on our own. Our qualification comes from God.

2 CORINTHIANS 3:5

God is more impressed by your faith than by your abilities. He uses your abilities only in proportion to your faith in him. If you want to delight God, say yes to him, walk in faith, and watch him accomplish great things through you. Abilities give you the *potential* for doing good; faith gives you the *power* to do good. Neither potential nor power alone is sufficient. They must work in harmony. When you use your God-given abilities, you will have a sense of satisfaction and feel fulfilled. So rejoice in your abilities, but let your rejoicing be poured out as an offering of thanks to the God who gave them. Without God, your abilities are dreams without power.

DIVINE PROMISE

ALL GLORY TO GOD, WHO IS ABLE, THROUGH
HIS MIGHTY POWER AT WORK WITHIN US,
TO ACCOMPLISH INFINITELY MORE THAN WE
MIGHT ASK OR THINK.   *Ephesians 3:20*

Absence

MY QUESTION *for* GOD

Why do I feel as if God is sometimes absent?

A MOMENT *with* GOD

O LORD, how long will you forget me? Forever? How
long will you look the other way? How long must I
struggle with anguish in my soul, with sorrow in my
heart every day? How long will my enemy have the
upper hand?   PSALM 13:1-2

Lord, through all the generations you have been
our home!   PSALM 90:1

[Jesus said,] "Teach these new disciples to obey all the
commands I have given you. And be sure of this: I am
with you always, even to the end of the age."

MATTHEW 28:20

The greater your troubles, the farther away God
sometimes seems. In your darkest hour, you may feel
that God has left you. In times like those, when it feels
as if God is absent, don't trust your feelings. Trust

God's promise that he will never leave you. Rely on what the Bible tells you is true, not on what your feelings are telling you. Even though you may feel as if God is far away, he really is always near. No matter how troubled you are, trust that God is with you. When you are hurting the most, he most wants to walk beside you.

DIVINE PROMISE

YOU KNOW WHEN I SIT DOWN OR STAND UP. YOU KNOW MY THOUGHTS EVEN WHEN I'M FAR AWAY. . . . I CAN NEVER ESCAPE FROM YOUR SPIRIT! I CAN NEVER GET AWAY FROM YOUR PRESENCE!   *Psalm 139:2, 7*

Absolutes

MY QUESTION *for* GOD

How does knowing that truth is absolute help me to live faithfully?

A MOMENT *with* GOD

In those days Israel had no king; all the people did whatever seemed right in their own eyes.   JUDGES 21:25

People may be right in their own eyes, but the LORD examines their heart.   PROVERBS 21:2

Your job is to obey the law, not to judge whether it applies to you.   JAMES 4:11

History is full of examples of individuals who did what was right in their own eyes—with catastrophic consequences for themselves and for others. Scripture teaches that you are born with the desire to sin; so doing your own thing will always lead you away from God, the source of all absolute truth. Your job is not to pass judgment on God's ways by devising your own, but to follow God and all he says. If you are trying a new recipe and you purposely stray from the instructions, your meal could turn out a disaster. It's the same with life. Follow God's instructions in the Bible, and life will work much better.

DIVINE PROMISE

ALL SCRIPTURE IS INSPIRED BY GOD AND IS USEFUL TO TEACH US WHAT IS TRUE AND TO MAKE US REALIZE WHAT IS WRONG IN OUR LIVES. IT CORRECTS US WHEN WE ARE WRONG AND TEACHES US TO DO WHAT IS RIGHT.
2 Timothy 3:16

Acceptance

MY QUESTION *for* GOD

How can I accept the difficulties that come into my life?

A MOMENT *with* GOD

Job replied, "You talk like a foolish woman. Should we accept only good things from the hand of God and never anything bad?"   JOB 2:10

To enjoy your work and accept your lot in life—this is indeed a gift from God.   ECCLESIASTES 5:19

You suffered along with those who were thrown into jail, and when all you owned was taken from you, you accepted it with joy. You knew there were better things waiting for you that will last forever.

HEBREWS 10:34

*Y*ou live in a fallen world. God told his followers to have realistic expectations about the world and to prepare for troubles that will come. Although you have hints of your glorious future in heaven, right now you live amid the continuing trials of life on earth. Accepting circumstances doesn't mean you have to like them. By keeping eternity in mind, you can grow from the difficulties you experience now, knowing that those difficulties will end with this earthly life. When you accept what comes from God's hand, you can trust that he has something to teach you through whatever comes your way.

DIVINE PROMISE

WHAT WE SUFFER NOW IS NOTHING COMPARED TO THE GLORY HE WILL REVEAL TO US LATER. . . . AND WE BELIEVERS ALSO GROAN, EVEN THOUGH WE HAVE THE HOLY SPIRIT WITHIN US AS A FORETASTE OF FUTURE GLORY, FOR WE LONG FOR OUR BODIES TO BE RELEASED FROM SIN AND SUFFERING. WE, TOO, WAIT WITH EAGER HOPE FOR THE DAY WHEN

GOD WILL GIVE US OUR FULL RIGHTS AS HIS
ADOPTED CHILDREN, INCLUDING THE NEW
BODIES HE HAS PROMISED US.   *Romans 8:18, 23*

Actions

MY QUESTION *for* GOD

How can my actions make me beautiful?

A MOMENT *with* GOD

Women who claim to be devoted to God should make
themselves attractive by the good things they do.

1 TIMOTHY 2:10

Even if some refuse to obey the Good News, your
godly lives will speak to them without any words.
They will be won over by observing your pure and
reverent lives. Don't be concerned about the outward
beauty of fancy hairstyles, expensive jewelry, or
beautiful clothes. You should clothe yourselves
instead with the beauty that comes from within, the
unfading beauty of a gentle and quiet spirit, which is
so precious to God. This is how the holy women of
old made themselves beautiful. They trusted God and
accepted the authority of their husbands.   1 PETER 3:1-5

Beautiful conduct is the fruit of godly thoughts and
godly character. A woman with godly character knows
her value in God's eyes and embraces the work he has

given her to do. There is nothing more beautiful than a woman at peace with God and confident in her God-given abilities and tasks. Her actions are beautiful because she gently meets the needs of others around her. When you work on cultivating your inward beauty, by focusing your attention on eternal matters and on what God says is most important, the beauty of your actions will encourage others and ring throughout eternity.

DIVINE PROMISE

CHARM IS DECEPTIVE, AND BEAUTY DOES NOT LAST; BUT A WOMAN WHO FEARS THE LORD WILL BE GREATLY PRAISED. *Proverbs 31:30*

Adaptability

MY QUESTION *for* GOD

How can I learn to adapt when life changes so quickly?

A MOMENT *with* GOD

God has made everything beautiful for its own time. He has planted eternity in the human heart, but even so, people cannot see the whole scope of God's work from beginning to end. ECCLESIASTES 3:11

It was by faith that Abraham obeyed when God called him to leave home and go to another land that God would give him as his inheritance. He went without knowing where he was going. HEBREWS 11:8

The ability to adapt goes hand in hand with trusting God. When you know that he loves you and trust that he has the best plans for your life, you can adapt willingly and quickly when the road of life takes a sudden sharp turn. You don't need to know all the details of God's plan for you in order to adapt to it. Full knowledge of all of the details is not necessary for obedience. Sometimes adapting means moving forward in faith and obedience to God and realizing that when he knows the way, you don't have to.

DIVINE PROMISE

DEAR BROTHERS AND SISTERS, WHEN TROUBLES COME YOUR WAY, CONSIDER IT AN OPPORTUNITY FOR GREAT JOY. FOR YOU KNOW THAT WHEN YOUR FAITH IS TESTED, YOUR ENDURANCE HAS A CHANCE TO GROW. SO LET IT GROW, FOR WHEN YOUR ENDURANCE IS FULLY DEVELOPED, YOU WILL BE PERFECT AND COMPLETE, NEEDING NOTHING.   *James 1:2-4*

Admirability

MY QUESTION *for* GOD

How can I be a woman that people admire and respect?

A MOMENT *with* GOD

Charm is deceptive, and beauty does not last; but a woman who fears the LORD will be greatly praised.

PROVERBS 31:30

*T*he most admirable qualities grow from having deep honor and respect for God. When you reflect God's character, you never need to put up a false front or be afraid of losing your "girlish figure" because you have qualities that others will admire long after your outer beauty has faded.

A sensible person wins admiration.   PROVERBS 12:8

Wisdom is better than foolishness, just as light is better than darkness.   ECCLESIASTES 2:13

*W*isdom and good sense are admirable qualities that steady your life. Being wise not only helps you to live a godly life, but it helps you to know how to guide others into godly living as well. When others see their lives falling apart, they will look to you for steadiness and wise advice.

As a result of your ministry, they will give glory to God. For your generosity to them and to all believers will prove that you are obedient to the Good News of Christ. And they will pray for you with deep affection because of the overflowing grace God has given to you.   2 CORINTHIANS 9:13-14

*T*he most admirable quality of all is reflecting God's love as you faithfully serve others. When you see them from God's perspective and love them as he does, you can offer God's gentle touch and demonstrate his love. You will always be admired by others who experience God through you.

DIVINE PROMISE

THERE WILL BE GLORY AND HONOR AND PEACE
FROM GOD FOR ALL WHO DO GOOD.   *Romans 2:10*

Adoption

MY QUESTION *for* GOD

How is adoption a picture of my relationship with God?

A MOMENT *with* GOD

To all who believed him and accepted him, he gave
the right to become children of God.   JOHN 1:12

When the right time came, God sent his Son, born
of a woman, subject to the law. God sent him to buy
freedom for us who were slaves to the law, so that he
could adopt us as his very own children. GALATIANS 4:4-5

Even before he made the world, God loved us and
chose us in Christ to be holy and without fault in his
eyes. God decided in advance to adopt us into his own
family by bringing us to himself through Jesus Christ.
This is what he wanted to do, and it gave him great
pleasure. So we praise God for the glorious grace he
has poured out on us who belong to his dear Son.

EPHESIANS 1:4-6

The process of adoption is a beautiful picture of God's
love for you. Just as adoptive parents make a choice to

give a child a new life, Jesus chose to give you a life you couldn't otherwise achieve. People who adopt children decide to lovingly teach and nurture them, and they give those children all of the rights and privileges of being a member of the family. As a child of God, you are privileged to receive all his blessings, in both this life and the next.

DIVINE PROMISE

I WILL BE YOUR FATHER, AND YOU WILL BE MY SONS AND DAUGHTERS, SAYS THE LORD ALMIGHTY.   *2 Corinthians 6:18*

Adversity

MY QUESTION *for* GOD

How does God's presence in my life strengthen me for coping with adversity?

A MOMENT *with* GOD

When you go through deep waters, I will be with you. When you go through rivers of difficulty, you will not drown. When you walk through the fire of oppression, you will not be burned up; the flames will not consume you.   ISAIAH 43:2

When you are faced with great adversity, you probably ask, "Where is God when I need him most?" The answer is always the same—he is right beside you. God is there, providing the power to help you cope. In this life, God doesn't promise to save you *from* trouble. In fact, Scripture says *"when* you go through deep waters," warning that in this life, adversity will come your way. It's the natural consequence of living in a fallen world. God will not act like a genie in a bottle, granting your every wish, because then you would follow him for the wrong reasons, and your character would never grow. Instead, God promises to be with you *in* your troubles, to give you wisdom to cope, strength to conquer your problems, and understanding to see how you will become stronger as you learn to deal with and overcome adversity.

DIVINE PROMISE

THE LORD HELPS THE FALLEN AND LIFTS THOSE BENT BENEATH THEIR LOADS.   *Psalm 145:14*

Advice

MY QUESTIONS *for* GOD

Do I really need advice from others? How do I know whether or not I'm getting good advice?

A MOMENT *with* GOD

Fools think their own way is right, but the wise listen to others.   PROVERBS 12:15

The instruction of the wise is like a life-giving
fountain; those who accept it avoid the snares
of death.   PROVERBS 13:14

Wise words are like deep waters; wisdom flows from
the wise like a bubbling brook.   PROVERBS 18:4

Timely advice is lovely, like golden apples in a
silver basket.   PROVERBS 25:11

𝒢ood advice is not merely helpful; it brings relief
when it comes to you at just the right moment. God
can use the advice of a trained counselor or even a conversation with a trusted friend as a turning point in
your life. He often allows the words of others to reach
you at the moment when you are most ready to receive
it. No one is wise enough to anticipate all the possibilities of a situation or to grasp all the issues related to
a problem. Refusing to listen to others is a sign that
you're not ready for change or spiritual growth. Right
counsel that is consistent with God's Word can make
the difference between success and failure, joy and sorrow, prosperity and poverty, victory and defeat. At the
critical moment, when you're most ready to hear it,
God's wisdom will penetrate your heart.

DIVINE PROMISE
TRUE WISDOM AND POWER ARE FOUND
IN GOD; COUNSEL AND UNDERSTANDING
ARE HIS. *Job 12:13*

Affection

MY QUESTION *for* GOD

How can I express my affection for God?

A MOMENT *with* GOD

Give to the LORD the glory he deserves! Bring your
offering and come into his presence. Worship the
LORD in all his holy splendor.   1 CHRONICLES 16:29

Shout with joy to the LORD, all the earth! Worship
the LORD with gladness. Come before him, singing
with joy. Acknowledge that the LORD is God! He
made us, and we are his. We are his people, the sheep
of his pasture. Enter his gates with thanksgiving; go
into his courts with praise. Give thanks to him and
praise his name.   PSALM 100:1-4

Because of your unfailing love, I can enter your house;
I will worship at your Temple with deepest awe.

PSALM 5:7

You express your affection for God through worship.
You can worship God anywhere, but these psalms focus
on the intentional worship that happened when people
gathered in the Temple to praise God with all their might.
Have you made a commitment to regular and true worship? When you worship, do you do so with your whole
being, body and soul? Imagine a spouse who never says,
"I love you," or rarely desires to be with you or never
speaks of you to others. True worship is not mumbling

a few hymns, sitting through a sermon, and then going home. It is an expression of your deepest devotion and affection for the God who loves you passionately.

DIVINE PROMISE

SURELY YOUR GOODNESS AND UNFAILING LOVE WILL PURSUE ME ALL THE DAYS OF MY LIFE.   *Psalm 23:6*

Affirmation

MY QUESTIONS *for* GOD

How does God affirm me? How do I know that he truly values my life?

A MOMENT *with* GOD

God created human beings in his own image. In the image of God he created them; male and female he created them.   GENESIS 1:27

Long ago the LORD said to Israel: "I have loved you, my people, with an everlasting love. With unfailing love I have drawn you to myself."   JEREMIAH 31:3

God loved the world so much that he gave his one and only Son, so that everyone who believes in him will not perish but have eternal life. God sent his Son into the world not to judge the world, but to save the world through him.   JOHN 3:16-17

You are living stones that God is building into his spiritual temple. What's more, you are his holy priests. Through the mediation of Jesus Christ, you offer spiritual sacrifices that please God.   1 PETER 2:5

𝒴ou can find affirmation in knowing that God chose to create you in his image and to be in relationship with him. God draws you to himself, even to the point of sacrificing his own son to die for you. Your life is the story of God pursuing you, rescuing you from your sin, and restoring you to who you *are*. Read God's words to you in the Bible, and think about all he has done to show you how much you matter to him. When you realize how fully God values you, his love breaks through the world's lies that try to tell you what you ought to be and encourages you to be the woman he created you to be.

DIVINE PROMISE

WE KNOW WHAT REAL LOVE IS BECAUSE JESUS GAVE UP HIS LIFE FOR US.   *1 John 3:16*

Angels

MY QUESTION *for* GOD

Do I have a guardian angel?

A MOMENT *with* GOD

[Jesus said,] "Beware that you don't look down on any of these little ones. For I tell you that in heaven their angels are always in the presence of my heavenly Father." MATTHEW 18:10

He will order his angels to protect you wherever you go. They will hold you up with their hands so you won't even hurt your foot on a stone. PSALM 91:11-12

Angels are only servants—spirits sent to care for people who will inherit salvation. HEBREWS 1:14

*A*ngels are supernatural beings whose main purpose is to worship God and serve him. In the Bible they often perform the role of messengers who deliver God's words to human beings. God uses his angels to counsel, guide, protect, minister to, rescue, fight for, and care for his people. Whether he assigns one specific angel to each person or uses his host of angels is his choice and your blessing. Thank God for the ways in which angels may have touched you. Chances are that angels have played a greater role in your life than you realize.

DIVINE PROMISE

THE ANGEL OF THE LORD IS A GUARD; HE SURROUNDS AND DEFENDS ALL WHO FEAR HIM. *Psalm 34:7*

Appreciation

MY QUESTION *for* GOD

*What is the importance of expressing my appreciation
to others?*

A MOMENT *with* GOD

Greet Apelles, a good man whom Christ approves.
And give my greetings to the believers from the
household of Aristobulus. Greet Herodion, my fellow
Jew. Greet the Lord's people from the household
of Narcissus. Give my greetings to Tryphena and
Tryphosa, the Lord's workers, and to dear Persis,
who has worked so hard for the Lord. Greet Rufus,
whom the Lord picked out to be his very own; and
also his dear mother, who has been a mother to me.

ROMANS 16:10-13

Every time I think of you, I give thanks to my God.
Whenever I pray, I make my requests for all of you
with joy.   PHILIPPIANS 1:3-4

You can probably still remember the worst thing
someone ever said to you. It has probably stayed with
you, and it may even still hurt. Can you remember the
best thing someone ever said to you? All of us could
stand to hear more words of appreciation and encouragement, so why not start by giving some to others?
Paul understood the importance of well-timed words
of appreciation. You can let others know that you ap-
preciate them by thanking them and building them

up. Notice what a difference a few words of appreciation can make! What you say to others may be the best words they've ever heard; it may even encourage them for a lifetime.

DIVINE PROMISE

I HAVE NOT STOPPED THANKING GOD FOR YOU. I PRAY FOR YOU CONSTANTLY. *Ephesians 1:16*

Assurance

MY QUESTION *for* GOD

How can my assurance of heaven transform the way I live today?

A MOMENT *with* GOD

[Jesus said,] "My sheep listen to my voice; I know them, and they follow me. I give them eternal life, and they will never perish. No one can snatch them away from me, for my Father has given them to me, and he is more powerful than anyone else. No one can snatch them from the Father's hand. The Father and I are one."   JOHN 10:27-30

You didn't choose me. I chose you. I appointed you to go and produce lasting fruit, so that the Father will give you whatever you ask for, using my name.

JOHN 15:16

I know the one in whom I trust, and I am sure that he is able to guard what I have entrusted to him until the day of his return.   2 TIMOTHY 1:12

𝒢od's promises about heaven are as certain as all of his other promises. When you've entrusted your life to God, he will certainly guard your eternal future because of his deep love for you. Ultimately, it is God's hold on you, not your grip on him, that matters most. You are saved by faith in him, not by your own efforts. Because of God's steadfast hold on you, you can be strong and courageous as you seek to obey him and follow where he leads in this life. And you can be confident in his promise of eternal life and the future he has planned for you that is far better than you can ever imagine! Live today as if you truly believe that, and see how your perspective changes.

DIVINE PROMISE

WHEN THE GREAT SHEPHERD APPEARS, YOU WILL RECEIVE A CROWN OF NEVER-ENDING GLORY AND HONOR.   1 Peter 5:4

Attitude

MY QUESTION for GOD

How does a positive attitude carry me through hard times?

A Moment *with* God

Don't worry about anything; instead, pray about
everything. Tell God what you need, and thank him
for all he has done.   PHILIPPIANS 4:6

I have learned how to be content with whatever I
have. I know how to live on almost nothing or with
everything. I have learned the secret of living in every
situation, whether it is with a full stomach or empty,
with plenty or little. For I can do everything through
Christ, who gives me strength.   PHILIPPIANS 4:11-13

Be thankful in all circumstances, for this is God's
will for you who belong to Christ Jesus.

1 THESSALONIANS 5:18

*H*ard times and life struggles are the raw materials
for God's mighty work in your life. Although it is hard
to be thankful *for* the tough times, you can learn to
be thankful *in* them. Your outlook on life determines
how you view your problems. If you see them only as
obstacles, you will tend to develop an attitude of bitterness, cynicism, and hopelessness. If you see them as
a crucible for strengthening your character and convic-
tions, you will learn to rise above them and even thank
God for how he is refining you through them.

DIVINE PROMISE

IF WE ARE TO SHARE [CHRIST'S] GLORY, WE
MUST ALSO SHARE HIS SUFFERING. YET WHAT
WE SUFFER NOW IS NOTHING COMPARED
TO THE GLORY HE WILL REVEAL TO US
LATER.   *Romans 8:17-18*

Balance

MY QUESTION *for* GOD

What are the blessings of a balanced life?

A MOMENT *with* GOD

Give according to what you have, not what you don't
have. Of course, I don't mean your giving should make
life easy for others and hard for yourselves. I only mean
that there should be some equality. Right now you have
plenty and can help those who are in need. Later, they
will have plenty and can share with you when you need
it. In this way, things will be equal.   2 CORINTHIANS 8:12-14

True godliness with contentment is itself great
wealth. After all, we brought nothing with us when
we came into the world, and we can't take anything
with us when we leave it. So if we have enough food
and clothing, let us be content. But people who long
to be rich fall into temptation and are trapped by
many foolish and harmful desires that plunge them
into ruin and destruction.   1 TIMOTHY 6:6-9

A key to finding satisfaction in life is the balance between meeting your own needs and the needs of others. Focusing too much on what you cannot have, should not have, or will never have breeds feelings of dissatisfaction. The more dissatisfied you are, the more you tend to focus only on yourself, which throws your life off balance. It's important to meet your own needs for food, shelter, and clothing, but focusing too much on yourself will cause you to neglect one of God's greatest mandates: to help others who are in need. As you balance meeting your own needs with meeting the needs of others, you will find contentment in caring for others and contentment with what you have.

DIVINE PROMISE
ENJOY PROSPERITY WHILE YOU CAN, BUT WHEN HARD TIMES STRIKE, REALIZE THAT BOTH COME FROM GOD.   *Ecclesiastes 7:14*

Beauty

MY QUESTION *for* GOD
How can I reflect the beauty of God?

A MOMENT *with* GOD

People judge by outward appearance, but the LORD looks at the heart.   1 SAMUEL 16:7

God has made everything beautiful for its own time.
ECCLESIASTES 3:11

Women who claim to be devoted to God should make themselves attractive by the good things they do.

1 TIMOTHY 2:10

Don't be concerned about the outward beauty of fancy hairstyles, expensive jewelry, or beautiful clothes. You should clothe yourselves instead with the beauty that comes from within, the unfading beauty of a gentle and quiet spirit, which is so precious to God.   1 PETER 3:3-4

*T*hings are loveliest and best when they are blooming in the right season. Life has many seasons, and every season can be the prime of life if you represent the season in which you are now living. The mature beauty of an older woman is quite different from that of a twenty-year-old with an attractive appearance. The beauty of an infant is different from the emerging beauty of an adolescent. Each has its seasonal beauty. The beauty of grace, sweetness, and charm transcends all of the seasons of life, although it may mature as one grows older. During all seasons, those who follow God reflect the beauty of his holiness, love, and wisdom. Combine all of these and behold beauty in symphony.

DIVINE PROMISE

OH, THE JOYS OF THOSE WHO DO NOT FOLLOW THE ADVICE OF THE WICKED, OR STAND AROUND WITH SINNERS, OR JOIN IN WITH MOCKERS. BUT THEY DELIGHT IN THE LAW OF THE LORD, MEDITATING ON IT DAY AND NIGHT.

THEY ARE LIKE TREES PLANTED ALONG THE
RIVERBANK, BEARING FRUIT EACH SEASON.
Psalm 1:1-3

Belonging

MY QUESTION *for* GOD

What are the privileges of belonging to God?

A MOMENT *with* GOD

Those who die in the LORD will live; their bodies
will rise again!   ISAIAH 26:19

Now that you belong to Christ, you are the true
children of Abraham. You are his heirs, and God's
promise to Abraham belongs to you.   GALATIANS 3:29

All praise to God, the Father of our Lord Jesus Christ,
who has blessed us with every spiritual blessing in the
heavenly realms because we are united with Christ.

 EPHESIANS 1:3

*B*elonging to God means that sin no longer has to
control you; you can overcome it. You will still sin,
but you are no longer enslaved to it. Belonging to God
also means that you can be certain that death is not
the end, that you will live eternally with God and receive all that he has promised his people in the Bible.
This includes blessings that you can experience today,
such as peace of heart, comfort, close friendships, and

the satisfaction of knowing that you are doing what
God has created you to do—just a few of the countless
privileges of belonging to God.

DIVINE PROMISE

I WILL WALK AMONG YOU; I WILL BE YOUR
GOD, AND YOU WILL BE MY PEOPLE.   *Leviticus 26:12*

Bible

MY QUESTION *for* GOD

What is the power of daily reading God's Word?

A MOMENT *with* GOD

The instructions of the LORD are perfect, reviving
the soul. The decrees of the LORD are trustworthy,
making wise the simple. The commandments of
the LORD are right, bringing joy to the heart. The
commands of the LORD are clear, giving insight
for living.   PSALM 19:7-8

Your laws please me; they give me wise advice.

PSALM 119:24

Your promise revives me; it comforts me in all
my troubles.   PSALM 119:50

All Scripture is inspired by God and is useful to teach
us what is true and to make us realize what is wrong
in our lives. It corrects us when we are wrong and

teaches us to do what is right. God uses it to prepare and equip his people to do every good work.

2 TIMOTHY 3:16-17

The word of God is alive and powerful. It is sharper than the sharpest two-edged sword, cutting between soul and spirit, between joint and marrow. It exposes our innermost thoughts and desires.   HEBREWS 4:12

God's Word, the Bible, is the only document that is "living." In other words, it is relevant for all people in all places in any time period. Because the Bible is a living document through which God speaks, daily reading is important so that God can communicate with you. It's easy to become distracted and lose touch with him. Reading God's Word every day keeps you in the presence of the One who created you for a purpose, who knows you best, and who can guide you along the best pathway for your life. If your heart is open to the words recorded in this book, you will begin to gain comfort, joy, insight, wisdom, knowledge, and the keys to living. You can experience daily divine moments with God, just by reading his Word!

DIVINE PROMISE

WHEN I DISCOVERED YOUR WORDS, I DEVOURED THEM. THEY ARE MY JOY AND MY HEART'S DELIGHT, FOR I BEAR YOUR NAME, O LORD GOD OF HEAVEN'S ARMIES.   *Jeremiah 15:16*

Blessings

MY QUESTION *for* GOD

How can I experience God's blessings?

A MOMENT *with* GOD

[God said,] "Not one of you from this wicked
generation will live to see the good land I swore
to give your ancestors, except Caleb. . . . He will
see this land because he has followed the LORD
completely.   DEUTERONOMY 1:35-36

It is good to give thanks to the LORD, to sing praises
to the Most High. It is good to proclaim your
unfailing love in the morning, your faithfulness
in the evening.   PSALM 92:1-2

Throughout the book of Deuteronomy runs a simple but profound principle: Obedience to God brings
blessings, and disobedience to God brings misfortune.
Be careful not to think of these blessings only in terms
of material possessions: The greatest blessings are far
more valuable than money or possessions. They come
in the form of joy, peace of heart, spiritual gifts, family,
friendships, and the confidence of eternal life. God has
given you far more than you realize—all of it undeserved, all of it given freely because he loves you. Your
obedience should not make you proud, as if you had
earned God's blessings. You haven't. Rather, your obedience should be the product of a heart thankful to God
for his undeserved blessings. Thanking him keeps you

aware of his blessings and keeps you from becoming ungrateful. A lack of gratitude is the first step toward missing out on God's blessings.

DIVINE PROMISE

LET'S NOT GET TIRED OF DOING WHAT IS GOOD. AT JUST THE RIGHT TIME WE WILL REAP A HARVEST OF BLESSING IF WE DON'T GIVE UP.

Galatians 6:9

Brokenness

MY QUESTION *for* GOD

Why is it so important to develop an attitude of brokenness?

A MOMENT *with* GOD

Have mercy on me, O God, because of your unfailing love. Because of your great compassion, blot out the stain of my sins. Wash me clean from my guilt. Purify me from my sin. For I recognize my rebellion; it haunts me day and night. Against you, and you alone, have I sinned; I have done what is evil in your sight. You will be proved right in what you say, and your judgment against me is just.   PSALM 51:1-4

The sacrifice you desire is a broken spirit. You will not reject a broken and repentant heart, O God.

PSALM 51:17

The experience of brokenness can be a divine moment with God. Brokenness comes most often in the midst of circumstances that overwhelm you or when sin reduces you to the point where you realize that the only way out of your mess is through God's help. It is a feeling of hitting bottom and realizing your utter dependence on God. Brokenness also comes as you grow in your awareness of God's holiness in contrast to your own sinfulness. It signifies the breaking point of your pride and self-sufficiency and becomes a turning point in your life. It results in a moment when you release control of your life to God's loving hands. God promises that when you are broken over the sin in your life, he will draw close to you, heal your self-inflicted wounds, and restore you to himself.

DIVINE PROMISE

THE LORD IS CLOSE TO THE BROKENHEARTED;
HE RESCUES THOSE WHOSE SPIRITS
ARE CRUSHED.   *Psalm 34:18*

Busyness

MY QUESTION *for* GOD

How can I overcome empty busyness?

A MOMENT *with* GOD

All our busy rushing ends in nothing.   PSALM 39:6

Plant your seed in the morning and keep busy all afternoon, for you don't know if profit will come from one activity or another—or maybe both.

ECCLESIASTES 11:6

Be careful how you live. Don't live like fools, but like those who are wise. Make the most of every opportunity in these evil days. Don't act thoughtlessly, but understand what the Lord wants you to do. . . . Be filled with the Holy Spirit

EPHESIANS 5:15-18

*R*ich harvests cannot come from idle hands. Getting a job done requires work. Busyness becomes dangerous only if your activities replace real accomplishment or if you are neglecting God or the people in your care. The key to overcoming empty busyness is to be fully productive for God. You do this by understanding his call and purpose for your life and prioritizing your activities around them. God empowers you to make the most of the time he's given you.

DIVINE PROMISE

TEACH US TO REALIZE THE BREVITY OF LIFE, SO THAT WE MAY GROW IN WISDOM. *Psalm 90:12*

Care

MY QUESTION *for* GOD

Where do I get the desire to help others?

A MOMENT *with* GOD

The LORD God placed the man in the Garden of Eden
to tend and watch over it.   GENESIS 2:15

I was naked, and you gave me clothing. I was sick, and
you cared for me. I was in prison, and you visited me.

                     MATTHEW 25:36

Be kind to each other, tenderhearted, forgiving one
another, just as God through Christ has forgiven you.

                     EPHESIANS 4:32

Pure and genuine religion in the sight of God the
Father means caring for orphans and widows in their
distress and refusing to let the world corrupt you.

                     JAMES 1:27

A caring spirit comes from the heart of God, whose
very nature is to care for others. God plants the seeds
of compassion and concern in the human heart, and
when need arises or tragedy strikes, those seeds quickly
grow to fruition. Anyone with a sense of compassion is
ready and willing to help another in need. Call it love,
concern, compassion, or care—it is your willingness
to reach out, to provide for others in a time of need, to
share with them, comfort them, and just be with them.

God's care for you is your model and inspiration for caring for others. As someone who bears God's image, you have the capacity to be moved with great compassion for another. Your love for God and gratitude for his care for you should drive you to act on that compassion. Your desire to care for others will grow out of your desire to please God and reflect his caring nature.

DIVINE PROMISE
I TELL YOU THE TRUTH, WHEN YOU DID
IT TO ONE OF THE LEAST OF THESE MY
BROTHERS AND SISTERS, YOU WERE DOING
IT TO ME! *Matthew 25:40*

Celebration

MY QUESTION *for* GOD

Why is it important to celebrate?

A MOMENT *with* GOD

On this day in early spring, in the month of Abib, you have been set free. You must celebrate this event. . . . You must explain to your children, "I am celebrating what the LORD did for me when I left Egypt."

EXODUS 13:4-5, 8

This festival will be a happy time of celebrating with your sons and daughters . . . to honor the LORD your God . . . for it is he who blesses you with bountiful harvests and gives you success in all your work.

DEUTERONOMY 16:14-15

Let us be glad and rejoice. . . . For the time has come
for the wedding feast of the Lamb.   REVELATION 19:7

*W*hen you think of celebration, you might think of
enjoying yourself and having a great time with others. You celebrate anniversaries, birthdays, victories,
promotions, awards, special milestones, marriages,
the birth of a new baby. But you also celebrate occasions such as the Lord's Supper, baptism, and other
solemn events. When you celebrate, you take time out
from your ordinary routine to observe and honor an
event that is notable, special, and important to you.
God gives you the best reason to celebrate because
he has rescued you from the consequences of sin and
shown you the way to heaven. Celebration is a powerful way to increase hope because it takes your focus
off your troubles and puts it on God's blessings and
on God himself. Those who love him have the most to
celebrate!

DIVINE PROMISE

LET ALL WHO TAKE REFUGE IN YOU REJOICE;
LET THEM SING JOYFUL PRAISES FOREVER.
SPREAD YOUR PROTECTION OVER THEM, THAT
ALL WHO LOVE YOUR NAME MAY BE FILLED
WITH JOY.   *Psalm 5:11*

Change

Where can I find the strength to change for the better?

A MOMENT *with* GOD

Create in me a clean heart, O God. Renew a loyal
spirit within me.   PSALM 51:10

Don't copy the behavior and customs of this world,
but let God transform you into a new person by
changing the way you think. Then you will learn to
know God's will for you, which is good and pleasing
and perfect.   ROMANS 12:2

Let the Spirit renew your thoughts and attitudes. Put
on your new nature, created to be like God—truly
righteous and holy.   EPHESIANS 4:23-24

Put on your new nature, and be renewed as you learn
to know your Creator and become like him.

COLOSSIANS 3:10

*I*t takes a long time to complete a great work of art.
The project goes through many stages from inspiration
to completion. You are God's work of art in process.
Although you may be fervent in a moment of faith, the
process of transformation into godliness takes a lifetime.
For real and dynamic change to occur, God has to give
you a new heart and a new way of thinking. His Spirit
will help you to focus on what is true and good and right.
Eventually you will begin to see the new you, a person

who displays God's good, holy, and true spirit. While these changes may appear slow to you, God's work is relentless and certain. Be patient with yourself and trust God to do his work in you at just the right pace.

DIVINE PROMISE

ANYONE WHO BELONGS TO CHRIST HAS BECOME A NEW PERSON. THE OLD LIFE IS GONE; A NEW LIFE HAS BEGUN!   *2 Corinthians 5:17*

Children

MY QUESTION *for* GOD

How can I teach my child about God's ways?

A MOMENT *with* GOD

I've also done it so you can tell your children and grandchildren about how I made a mockery of the Egyptians and about the signs I displayed among them—and so you will know that I am the LORD.

EXODUS 10:2

[Moses said,] "Commit yourselves wholeheartedly to these words of mine. Tie them to your hands and wear them on your forehead as reminders. Teach them to your children. Talk about them when you are at home and when you are on the road, when you are going to bed and when you are getting up."

DEUTERONOMY 11:18-19

Joshua said to the Israelites, "In the future your children will ask, 'What do these stones mean?' Then you can tell them, 'This is where the Israelites crossed the Jordan on dry ground.'"   JOSHUA 4:21-22

*G*od wants you to teach your children about him. One way to do this is to respond to a child's natural curiosity to God. When your child asks about a tree or a caterpillar, be ready to turn that question into a teaching moment. Explain how a tree or caterpillar or any creation is a gift from God the Creator. God commanded the Israelites to set up a memorial that would attract a child's curiosity and create teaching moments for the Israelite parents. You can create teaching moments for your children by setting up reminders of God in your home. These give you opportunities to share with your children about what God has done in your life and what he is doing in your child's life. The next time your child asks you to tell a story, share a time when God has worked in your life, blessed you, or forgiven you. This will show that God is real and willing to work in your children's lives as well.

DIVINE PROMISE

[GOD SAID,] "MY SPIRIT WILL NOT LEAVE THEM, AND NEITHER WILL THESE WORDS I HAVE GIVEN YOU. THEY WILL BE ON YOUR LIPS AND ON THE LIPS OF YOUR CHILDREN AND YOUR CHILDREN'S CHILDREN FOREVER." *Isaiah 59:21*

Children

MY QUESTION *for* GOD

What can children teach me about God?

A MOMENT *with* GOD

[Jesus said,] "I tell you the truth, unless you turn from your sins and become like little children, you will never get into the Kingdom of Heaven. So anyone who becomes as humble as this little child is the greatest in the Kingdom of Heaven." MATTHEW 18:3-4

[Jesus told his disciples,] "Let the children come to me. Don't stop them! For the Kingdom of God belongs to those who are like these children. I tell you the truth, anyone who doesn't receive the Kingdom of God like a child will never enter it." MARK 10:14-15

Jesus was filled with the joy of the Holy Spirit, and he said, "O Father, Lord of heaven and earth, thank you for hiding these things from those who think themselves wise and clever, and for revealing them to the childlike. Yes, Father, it pleased you to do it this way." LUKE 10:21

*C*hildren demonstrate the kind of innocence, curiosity, and faith that is so dear to God. They approach life eager to experience new adventures and learn about the world around them, and they trust their parents to be there to guide and comfort them and meet their needs. God wants his children to approach life the same way.

He is delighted when we are willing to follow him on the adventure of life, learn all we can about him, and trust him for all we need. Adults often tend to make life too complicated, but Jesus welcomes you to simply trust him and anticipate with delight the blessings of divine moments with him.

DIVINE PROMISE

YOU WILL TAKE DELIGHT IN THE ALMIGHTY AND LOOK UP TO GOD. *Job 22:26*

Choices

MY QUESTION *for* GOD

How can I be certain that the choices I make are in line with God's ways?

A MOMENT *with* GOD

Love the LORD your God, walk in all his ways, obey his commands, hold firmly to him, and serve him with all your heart and all your soul.   JOSHUA 22:5

[Joshua said,] "Choose today whom you will serve. . . . As for me and my family, we will serve the LORD."

JOSHUA 24:15

I have hidden your word in my heart, that I might not sin against you.   PSALM 119:11

There is safety in having many advisers.   PROVERBS 11:14

*E*very day presents new choices. The choice that you can always make—and only you can make—is to honor God and obey his Word. This decision will always point you toward God's ways and put you squarely in the center of his will. The best things to do to help you make good choices—and to avoid making choices that benefit you at others' expense—are to read God's Word, seek his guidance in prayer, and seek the advice of godly counselors. It is not complicated, but it is a challenge to put God and others ahead of everything else. Each day offers the choice to serve the Lord, but by following these guidelines and maintaining a "God first" attitude, you will usually know with certainty the quality of your decisions.

DIVINE PROMISE

[THE LORD] GUIDES ME ALONG RIGHT PATHS, BRINGING HONOR TO HIS NAME.   *Psalm 23:3*

Church

MY QUESTION *for* GOD

How can I experience God by going to church?

A MOMENT *with* GOD

The one thing I ask of the LORD—the thing I seek most—is to live in the house of the LORD all the days of my life, delighting in the LORD's perfections and meditating in his Temple.   PSALM 27:4

What joy for those who can live in your house, always
singing your praises.   PSALM 84:4

*E*ven though God lives in the heart of every believer,
he also lives in the community of the church. When the
church is gathered together, God is there in a special
way. Just as actually being at a concert or sports event
is much more exciting than watching it on television,
participating with other believers in worship is so much
more meaningful than worshiping only by yourself.

Just as our bodies have many parts and each part has
a special function, so it is with Christ's body. We
are many parts of one body, and we all belong to
each other.   ROMANS 12:4-5

*G*od has given every believer special gifts. Some people
are great organizers or administrators; others are gifted
musicians, teachers, or dishwashers! When the members of a congregation use their gifts to serve, the church
becomes a powerful force for good, a strong witness
for Jesus, and a mighty army to combat Satan's attacks
against God's people. The church needs you, for the
body of Christ is not complete unless you are there!

Let us not neglect our meeting together, as some
people do, but encourage one another, especially
now that the day of his return is drawing near.

                                                        HEBREWS 10:25

$\mathcal{G}$ood friends are a wonderful gift, but fellowship at church among other believers is unique because almighty God is present there. The church brings people together who have a common perspective on life. Christian fellowship provides a place of honest sharing about the things that really matter, encouragement to stay strong in the face of temptation and persecution, and God's wisdom for dealing with problems.

DIVINE PROMISE

[JESUS SAID,] "WHERE TWO OR THREE GATHER TOGETHER AS MY FOLLOWERS, I AM THERE AMONG THEM." *Matthew 18:20*

Circumstances

MY QUESTION *for* GOD

How can I experience God in the midst of troubling circumstances?

A MOMENT *with* GOD

Though the fig trees have no blossoms, and there are no grapes on the vines; even though the olive crop fails, and the fields lie empty and barren; even though the flocks die in the fields, and the cattle barns are empty, yet I will rejoice in the LORD! I will be joyful in the God of my salvation! The Sovereign LORD is my strength! He makes me as surefooted as a deer, able to tread upon the heights. HABAKKUK 3:17-19

*F*ocus less on your troubles and more on the joy, peace, and future that come from a relationship with God. You can always respond joyfully to the God who offers you the eternal gift of salvation. The more you wallow in the difficulty of unpleasant circumstances, the more they may drag you under. The more you reach out to God, the more he can lift you up.

In that way, you will be acting as true children of your Father in heaven. For he gives his sunlight to both the evil and the good, and he sends rain on the just and the unjust alike.   MATTHEW 5:45

Be thankful in all circumstances, for this is God's will for you who belong to Christ Jesus.

1 THESSALONIANS 5:18

*A*ccept life's circumstances with thanksgiving to God, and trust in him for his constant presence and comfort. Whether you are currently living in sunshine or rain, God never changes, and his love for you never changes. God is always eager to teach you something from both the good and the bad.

Don't worry about anything; instead, pray about everything. Tell God what you need, and thank him for all he has done.   PHILIPPIANS 4:6

*R*efuse to worry. One of the hardest lessons of life to learn is to turn worry into confident prayer when bad circumstances come your way. Come to God with your needs in thanksgiving for what he has done for

you, and trust that he will bring good fruit out of the
difficult times.

DIVINE PROMISE

LIGHT SHINES IN THE DARKNESS FOR THE
GODLY. THEY ARE GENEROUS, COMPASSIONATE,
AND RIGHTEOUS. . . . SUCH PEOPLE WILL NOT
BE OVERCOME BY EVIL. THOSE WHO ARE
RIGHTEOUS WILL BE LONG REMEMBERED. THEY
DO NOT FEAR BAD NEWS; THEY CONFIDENTLY
TRUST THE LORD TO CARE FOR THEM. THEY
ARE CONFIDENT AND FEARLESS AND CAN FACE
THEIR FOES TRIUMPHANTLY.   *Psalm 112:4, 6-8*

Comfort

MY QUESTION *for* GOD

How does God speak comfort to me in difficult times?

A MOMENT *with* GOD

In my distress I prayed to the LORD, and the LORD
answered me and set me free.   PSALM 118:5

I meditate on your age-old regulations; O LORD, they
comfort me.   PSALM 119:52

*Y*our need for comfort and God's supply of comfort
are always in perfect balance. God welcomes those who
call on him in distress. He always answers the cry of the
person who is lonely, distressed, or afraid. God loves

to show his power in your weakness. Since God is your source of comfort, his Word is your greatest resource for finding it. God's promises in the Bible comfort and encourage you in this life and give you confident assurance of one day living forever in peace and security with him. God's Word is as close as your fingertips, and God himself is as close as your whispered prayer.

DIVINE PROMISE

EVERY WORD OF GOD PROVES TRUE. HE
IS A SHIELD TO ALL WHO COME TO HIM
FOR PROTECTION. *Proverbs 30:5*

Comfort

MY QUESTION *for* GOD

In times of distress, how will I experience God's comfort?

A MOMENT *with* GOD

Whenever they were in trouble and turned to the LORD . . . and sought him out, they found him.

2 CHRONICLES 15:4

The LORD is good, a strong refuge when trouble comes. He is close to those who trust in him. NAHUM 1:7

God doesn't always act in the way you might expect. You might expect him to comfort you by providing things that you think you want or need, but the Bible says that often God comforts you with his presence, not with provisions. Things are temporary, but God is eternal. Your needs and wants are constantly changing. Material provisions can provide comfort for a time, but God is the only source of comfort at *all* times. Every time you need comfort, God shows up, not with presents, but with his abiding presence.

DIVINE PROMISE

DON'T BE AFRAID, FOR I AM WITH YOU.
DON'T BE DISCOURAGED, FOR I AM YOUR GOD.
I WILL STRENGTHEN YOU AND HELP YOU.
I WILL HOLD YOU UP WITH MY VICTORIOUS
RIGHT HAND.   *Isaiah 41:10*

Commitment

MY QUESTION *for* GOD

What does it take to be truly committed to God?

A MOMENT *with* GOD

Fear the LORD and serve him wholeheartedly.

JOSHUA 24:14

If we are thrown into the blazing furnace, the God whom we serve is able to save us. . . . But even if he doesn't, we want to make it clear to you, Your Majesty, that we will never serve your gods.

DANIEL 3:17-18

Jesus called out to them, "Come, follow me, and I will show you how to fish for people!" And they left their nets at once and followed him.   MATTHEW 4:19-20

Give yourselves completely to God, for you were dead, but now you have new life. So use your whole body as an instrument to do what is right for the glory of God.   ROMANS 6:13

*C*ommitment is more than intellectual agreement; it involves giving your whole self—body, soul, emotions, and mind—to God for his use. Commitment requires a decision of the mind followed by an act of the will to follow through regardless of the difficulty or the cost. Commitment to God can be costly, but God promises great blessings for those who are faithful in their commitment to him.

DIVINE PROMISE

COMMIT EVERYTHING YOU DO TO THE LORD. TRUST HIM, AND HE WILL HELP YOU.   *Psalm 37:5*

Commitment

MY QUESTION *for* GOD

Is there a cost to being committed to God?

A MOMENT *with* GOD

[Jesus said,] "If you want to be my disciple, you must
hate everyone else by comparison—your father and
mother, wife and children, brothers and sisters—yes,
even your own life. Otherwise, you cannot be my
disciple. And if you do not carry your own cross
and follow me, you cannot be my disciple. But don't
begin until you count the cost. For who would begin
construction of a building without first calculating
the cost to see if there is enough money to finish it?"

LUKE 14:26-28

Could Jesus really have been telling us to turn our
backs on our families? Of course not! We can understand the apparent harshness of his words only when
we grasp the nature of commitment. Jesus wants us
to see that commitment is exclusive and costly. People
fully devoted to becoming professional musicians cannot also be fully dedicated to becoming professional
athletes without compromising their commitments to
one or the other. In the same way, Jesus must become
the central and dominating commitment of our lives,
and we must consider all other loves in light of our
commitment to him. We will make financial decisions
based on biblical principles instead of buying whatever
we want. We may make sacrifices to take in a needy
family, even though it puts additional strain on our own
family. Think about your commitment. Is it diluted
by your overcommitment to other activities or loves?
Evaluate all your commitments by asking, "Is this wor-

thy of my time and affection in light of my complete
commitment to Jesus?"

DIVINE PROMISE

IF WE ARE FAITHFUL TO THE END . . . WE WILL
SHARE IN ALL THAT BELONGS TO CHRIST.
Hebrews 3:14

Community

MY QUESTION *for* GOD

How can I have the greatest impact on my community?

A MOMENT *with* GOD

There was a believer in Joppa named Tabitha. . . . She
was always doing kind things for others and helping
the poor.   ACTS 9:36

Owe nothing to anyone—except for your obligation
to love one another. If you love your neighbor, you
will fulfill the requirements of God's law.   ROMANS 13:8

Be careful to live properly among your unbelieving
neighbors. Then even if they accuse you of doing
wrong, they will see your honorable behavior,
and they will give honor to God when he judges
the world.   1 PETER 2:12

You must worship Christ as Lord of your life. And
if someone asks about your Christian hope, always

be ready to explain it. But do this in a gentle and
respectful way. Keep your conscience clear. Then if
people speak against you, they will be ashamed when
they see what a good life you live because you belong
to Christ.   1 PETER 3:15-16

God's influence in your life can be very attractive to
others. The more you reflect God's loving character,
the more people will be drawn to you. Practically, this
may mean just being a friendly neighbor, volunteer-
ing to serve the needy in your community, being a responsible citizen, making peace with difficult people,
or treating others with fairness and respect. Through
these simple actions you can be an attractive example of
God's love to people in your community. With God's
power, your character can become a beacon of light
that brightens the whole community with God's trans-
forming ways. Although you will sometimes make mistakes, live so your neighbors can say, "We can plainly
see that God is with you."

DIVINE PROMISE

[JESUS SAID,] "YOU ARE THE LIGHT OF THE
WORLD. . . . NO ONE LIGHTS A LAMP AND THEN
PUTS IT UNDER A BASKET. INSTEAD, A LAMP IS
PLACED ON A STAND, WHERE IT GIVES LIGHT
TO EVERYONE IN THE HOUSE. IN THE SAME
WAY, LET YOUR GOOD DEEDS SHINE OUT FOR
ALL TO SEE, SO THAT EVERYONE WILL PRAISE
YOUR HEAVENLY FATHER.   *Matthew 5:14-16*

Comparisons

MY QUESTION *for* GOD

How can God help me resist the need to compare myself to others?

A MOMENT *with* GOD

Oh, that my actions would consistently reflect your decrees! Then I will not be ashamed when I compare my life with your commands.   PSALM 119:5-6

Why do you condemn another believer? Why do you look down on another believer? Remember, we will all stand before the judgment seat of God. . . . Yes, each of us will give a personal account to God.

ROMANS 14:10, 12

These other men . . . are only comparing themselves with each other, using themselves as the standard of measurement. How ignorant!   2 CORINTHIANS 10:12

Pay careful attention to your own work, for then you will get the satisfaction of a job well done, and you won't need to compare yourself to anyone else. For we are each responsible for our own conduct.

GALATIANS 6:4-5

"How do I measure up?" is a question most of us grapple with. Satan will try to convince you that your worth is based on how you measure up in comparison with others in appearance, possessions, accomplishments, or social status. This will usually leave you feeling either inadequate and envious or full of pride. A better method of determining your worth is comparing yourself with God's standards. Measured against his holiness, everyone falls short and is humbled; but in God's eyes, every person is valued and loved. Maintaining a balance between humility over your sin and exulting in God's lavish grace is a healthy way to live. God doesn't compare you with others, so neither should you. Enjoy his grace, which has no comparison, and bask in the gracious ways that God shows his love to you.

DIVINE PROMISE

YES, EVERYTHING ELSE IS WORTHLESS WHEN COMPARED WITH THE INFINITE VALUE OF KNOWING CHRIST JESUS MY LORD. FOR HIS SAKE I HAVE DISCARDED EVERYTHING ELSE, COUNTING IT ALL AS GARBAGE, SO THAT I COULD GAIN CHRIST. *Philippians 3:8*

Compassion

MY QUESTION *for* GOD

How can I reflect Christ's compassion in ways that touch others?

A MOMENT *with* GOD

Jesus saw the huge crowd as he stepped from the boat, and he had compassion on them because they were like sheep without a shepherd.   MARK 6:34

When the Lord saw her, his heart overflowed with
compassion. "Don't cry!" he said.   LUKE 7:13

$\mathscr{C}$ompassion is both an emotion and an action. It is a
litmus test of your commitment and desire to love others as Christ loves you. When your heart truly aches
for another, you get an idea of how the needs of all
humanity moved Jesus to die on the cross. If you're not
moved by the incredible needs and pain around you,
you are either too self-focused or in danger of developing a heart of stone that is unresponsive to either God
or others. Compassion motivates you to put your love
into action to meet the needs of others, particularly
those who cannot help themselves. You can pass along
the compassion of Christ by your willingness to care
for others around you. A compassionate heart is a mark
of godliness.

DIVINE PROMISE

THE LORD IS GOOD TO EVERYONE. HE SHOWERS
COMPASSION ON ALL HIS CREATION.   *Psalm 145:9*

$\mathscr{C}$ompatibility

MY QUESTION *for* GOD

How am I compatible with God?

A Moment *with* God

I will give you a new heart, and I will put a new spirit in you. I will take out your stony, stubborn heart and give you a tender, responsive heart. And I will put my Spirit in you so that you will follow my decrees and be careful to obey my regulations.   EZEKIEL 36:26-27

We have received God's Spirit (not the world's spirit), so we can know the wonderful things God has freely given us.   1 CORINTHIANS 2:12

People who aren't spiritual can't receive these truths from God's Spirit. It all sounds foolish to them and they can't understand it, for only those who are spiritual can understand what the Spirit means. . . . But we understand these things, for we have the mind of Christ.   1 CORINTHIANS 2:14-16

*W*hen you believe in and obey God, his Holy Spirit works in you to change your interests and desires to match God's interests and desires. The more the Holy Spirit works in your life, the more compatible you are with God and the more you can enjoy the experience of God at work within you.

DIVINE PROMISE

ALL OF US WHO HAVE HAD THAT VEIL REMOVED CAN SEE AND REFLECT THE GLORY OF THE LORD. AND THE LORD—WHO IS THE SPIRIT—MAKES US MORE AND MORE LIKE HIM AS WE ARE CHANGED INTO HIS GLORIOUS IMAGE. *2 Corinthians 3:18*

Complacency

MY QUESTION *for* GOD

How can I combat complacent inaction?

A MOMENT *with* GOD

In his unfailing love, my God will stand with me. He will let me look down in triumph on all my enemies. Don't kill them, for my people soon forget such lessons; stagger them with your power, and bring them to their knees, O Lord our shield.   PSALM 59:10-11

If you think you are standing strong, be careful not to fall.   1 CORINTHIANS 10:12

Stay alert! Watch out for your great enemy, the devil. He prowls around like a roaring lion, looking for someone to devour. Stand firm against him, and be strong in your faith.   1 PETER 5:8-9

In Psalm 59, David prays that God will not destroy Israel's enemies. It sounds like a strange request. Why? Because David knows that absence of enemies will lead the Israelites to become spiritually complacent. It was the threat of attack that kept them dependent on God.

Feeling invulnerable is spiritually unhealthy for you, too. Problems and trials keep you spiritually sharp and fully dependent on God. During good times, be alert to the constant threat of temptation, and remember that health, relationships, financial stability, and all other earthly blessings can vanish in an instant. The fragility of life prompts faith, and faith in God is your only true security.

DIVINE PROMISE

LORD, WHERE DO I PUT MY HOPE? MY ONLY HOPE IS IN YOU. *Psalm 39:7*

Compliments

MY QUESTION *for* GOD

How can my compliments help others experience God?

A MOMENT *with* GOD

As we pray to our God and Father about you, we think of your faithful work, your loving deeds, and the enduring hope you have because of our Lord Jesus Christ. 1 THESSALONIANS 1:3

I always thank my God when I pray for you, Philemon, because I keep hearing about your faith in the Lord Jesus and your love for all of God's people. And I am praying that you will put into action the generosity that comes from your faith as you understand and experience all the good things we have in Christ. Your love has given me much joy and comfort, my brother, for your kindness has often refreshed the hearts of God's people. PHILEMON: 1:4-7

$\mathcal{C}$omplimenting others can lead you to praise God for his work in their lives. When you notice others' strengths or spiritual growth, you may be offering them just the encouragement they need. How often have others' compliments to you helped you clarify where God wants you to be? Compliments are divine moments of encouragement when we offer them sincerely out of a pure and tender heart.

DIVINE PROMISE

WHEN PEOPLE COMMEND THEMSELVES, IT DOESN'T COUNT FOR MUCH. THE IMPORTANT THING IS FOR THE LORD TO COMMEND THEM.

2 Corinthians 10:18

$\mathcal{C}$onfession

MY QUESTION *for* GOD

How does confession help me to experience God's forgiveness?

A MOMENT *with* GOD

When you become aware of your guilt in any of these ways, you must confess your sin.   LEVITICUS 5:5

People who conceal their sins will not prosper, but if they confess and turn from them, they will receive mercy.   PROVERBS 28:13

Confession indicates your desire to have your sins forgiven. God often uses the feeling of guilt in your conscience to help you know it is time to apologize or confess wrongdoing. Do you feel guilty about something you have said or done to hurt another person? Perhaps God is prompting you to apologize and seek forgiveness. You should also ask God to reveal actions and thoughts that you aren't even aware displease him. What results from confession? God removes your guilt, restores your joy and willing obedience, and heals your broken soul with his forgiving love.

DIVINE PROMISE

IF WE CONFESS OUR SINS TO HIM, HE IS
FAITHFUL AND JUST TO FORGIVE US OUR SINS
AND TO CLEANSE US FROM ALL WICKEDNESS.
1 John 1:9

Confidence

MY QUESTION *for* GOD

*Where can I find the confidence I need to face life
without fear?*

A MOMENT *with* GOD

Good comes to those who lend money generously and conduct their business fairly. Such people will not be overcome by evil. Those who are righteous will be long remembered. They do not fear bad news; they confidently trust the LORD to care for them. They are confident and fearless and can face their foes triumphantly.

PSALM 112:5-8

Blessed are those who trust in the LORD and have made the LORD their hope and confidence.

JEREMIAH 17:7

I can do everything through Christ, who gives me strength.

PHILIPPIANS 4:13

Confidence can go down two tracks: It can lead to cockiness, which results in pride and boasting, or it can lead to an inner assurance, which produces a healthy self-esteem and a sure conviction of where you are going. Confidence that leads to cockiness brings with it many fears, the greatest of which is the fear of losing face in front of others. Confidence that leads to inner assurance is not pride; it is security in Christ. You are secure because God has called you for a specific purpose, and he has given you spiritual gifts to carry out that purpose. You are doing your best at what God has specifically called you to do. The Bible uses the word *boldness* for "confidence." With Christ by your side, you can boldly set out to do his work, confident that you are within his will.

DIVINE PROMISE

THE LORD IS MY LIGHT AND MY SALVATION— SO WHY SHOULD I BE AFRAID? *Psalm 27:1*

Conformity

MY QUESTION for GOD

What is the beauty of conformity to God's ways?

A MOMENT with GOD

Don't copy the behavior and customs of this world,
but let God transform you into a new person by
changing the way you think. Then you will learn to
know God's will for you, which is good and pleasing
and perfect.   ROMANS 12:2

You must be careful so that your freedom does not
cause others with a weaker conscience to stumble.

                                        1 CORINTHIANS 8:9

A potter shapes a plain lump of clay into his design,
conforming it to his idea of how it should look and
function. Society does the same thing to people. It has
a way of molding us to its way of looking, thinking,
and behaving. Unfortunately, culture rarely values
what God does, especially in the area of morality, so
conformity to God's ways is usually countercultural.
Many people say, "I'm going to do what I want. I don't
care what people say." But if you believe in God, your
task is to conform to God's way of thinking and acting,
even when it goes against what's popular. You have a
special responsibility to act as a representative of God.
If your actions are not consistent with your faith, then
you could cause others to question the life-changing
power of God. But your conformity to God's ways re-

veals your freedom from the influence of the culture. Your behavior should cause others to ask about your faith as they see you living out God's ways.

DIVINE PROMISE

O LORD, YOU ARE OUR FATHER. WE ARE THE CLAY, AND YOU ARE THE POTTER. WE ALL ARE FORMED BY YOUR HAND. *Isaiah 64:8*

Conscience

MY QUESTION *for* GOD

How can I have a clear conscience?

A MOMENT *with* GOD

Learn to know the God of your ancestors intimately. Worship and serve him with your whole heart and a willing mind. For the LORD sees every heart and knows every plan and thought. 1 CHRONICLES 28:9

May the words of my mouth and the meditation of my heart be pleasing to you, O LORD, my rock and my redeemer. PSALM 19:14

My conscience is clear, but that doesn't prove I'm right. It is the Lord himself who will examine me and decide. 1 CORINTHIANS 4:4

*W*hen your motives are selfish or impure, it is only a matter of time before your actions are also selfish and impure. God is far more concerned about the condition of your heart than he is about your external behavior, because your behavior always flows from your heart, not the other way around. Remember that God alone knows your heart. You may be able to fool others and yourself, but you can't fool God. Welcome his examination. Then you can say, like Paul, that your conscience is clear. And when your conscience is clear, your heart is open to God doing a great work in you and through you.

DIVINE PROMISE

YOUR WORD IS A LAMP TO GUIDE MY FEET AND A LIGHT FOR MY PATH.   *Psalm 119:105*

Contentment

MY QUESTION *for* GOD

What is the key to contentment in life?

A MOMENT *with* GOD

Satisfy us each morning with your unfailing love, so we may sing for joy to the end of our lives.   PSALM 90:14

I have learned how to be content with whatever I have. I know how to live on almost nothing or with everything. I have learned the secret of living in every situation, whether it is with a full stomach or empty, with plenty or little. For I can do everything through Christ, who gives me strength.   PHILIPPIANS 4:11-13

*C*ontentment is among life's most elusive qualities. The answer to the question "How much is enough?" always seems to be "Just a little bit more." Your deepest contentment and joy come not from the pursuit of happiness, pleasure, or material possessions but from the pursuit of intimacy with God. When you depend on material wealth, it means you're trying to build your own security, which leads you to crave more. The more you crave, the less satisfied you will be. But God has promised you that he is sufficient. Over and over the Bible teaches that human beings are most fully satisfied as they experience God's unfailing love. As you receive his provision in times of need, your security is built on the everlasting God, and you find yourself thankfully content rather than asking for more in times of plenty or want.

DIVINE PROMISE

EACH TIME [GOD] SAID, "MY GRACE IS ALL YOU NEED."   *2 Corinthians 12:9*

Conversation

MY QUESTION *for* GOD

How can I live my life in conversation with God?

A MOMENT *with* GOD

My God gave me the idea to call together all the
nobles and leaders of the city, along with the ordinary
citizens, for registration.   NEHEMIAH 7:5

Be careful that you do not refuse to listen to the
One who is speaking. For if the people of Israel did
not escape when they refused to listen to Moses, the
earthly messenger, we will certainly not escape if we
reject the One who speaks to us from heaven!

                                                         HEBREWS 12:25

Nehemiah gave God credit for the idea of register-
ing the people. This is different from the way some
people say, "The Lord told me ..." in order to support their plans or opinions. Rather, Nehemiah lived
with a constant sense of God's presence. His life was
a moment-by-moment conversation with God, even as
he pursued his energetic and ambitious agenda. How
can you grow more aware of God's speaking in your
life? You might try a Post-it note on your computer to
remind you to breathe a quick prayer whenever you sit
down to work. Or set your cell phone alarm to sound
every sixty minutes, and then take thirty seconds to
review how the Lord has been with you the last hour
and ask him to help you in the hour ahead. Take time to
listen to God too. One-sided conversations are boring.
When you take time to listen to God, your relationship grows. Spiritual growth is not hindered by God's
nonattendance but by your inattention. What are some

other ways your life can become a moment-by-moment conversation with God?

DIVINE PROMISE

COME AND LISTEN TO MY COUNSEL. I'LL SHARE
MY HEART WITH YOU AND MAKE YOU WISE.
Proverbs 1:23

Courage

MY QUESTION *for* GOD

Why doesn't God take away the things I am most afraid of?

A MOMENT *with* GOD

Having hope will give you courage.   JOB 11:18

All the believers lifted their voices together in prayer.
. . . "O Lord, hear their threats, and give us, your
servants, great boldness in preaching your word.
Stretch out your hand with healing power; may
miraculous signs and wonders be done through the
name of your holy servant Jesus." After this prayer,
the meeting place shook, and they were all filled with
the Holy Spirit. Then they preached the word of God
with boldness.   ACTS 4:24, 29-31

The early church was constantly threatened with persecution. The believers did not pray for the threats to

end, but for the courage to face them. Sometimes God will remove the things that frighten you. But more often, the Holy Spirit gives you the boldness to turn those threats into opportunities for spiritual growth and for declaring your faith. If God took away everything that frightened you, there would be no need for hope in your life. And it is hope that helps you see beyond the immediate crisis, causing you to place your current problem as well as your eternal future in God's hands. When you are afraid at the enormity of the problem facing you, it is a divine moment to recognize God right by your side.

DIVINE PROMISE

BE STRONG AND COURAGEOUS! DO NOT
BE AFRAID OR DISCOURAGED. FOR THE
LORD YOUR GOD IS WITH YOU WHEREVER
YOU GO.   *Joshua 1:9*

Creativity

MY QUESTION *for* GOD

How can the workmanship of God spark my own creativity?

A MOMENT *with* GOD

The heavens proclaim the glory of God. The skies display his craftsmanship. Day after day they continue to speak; night after night they make him known. They speak without a sound or word; their voice is never heard. Yet their message has gone throughout the earth, and their words to all the world. PSALM 19:1-4

Beautiful words stir my heart. I will recite a lovely poem about the king, for my tongue is like the pen of a skillful poet. PSALM 45:1

There will be an abundance of flowers and singing and joy! The deserts will become as green as the mountains of Lebanon, as lovely as Mount Carmel or the plain of Sharon. There the LORD will display his glory, the splendor of our God. ISAIAH 35:2

All nature sings and displays beauty that surpasses the finest music, poetry, or creative genius of all human artists put together. God the Creator is a God of design, color, plan, organization, beauty, magnificence, and order. The great art of the world only copies his creation. The finest model of craftsmanship and artistic skill is found in the creation of the universe. Your own creativity is the overflow of a heart and mind filled with the good things of God. If you're looking for a little inspiration or motivation, fill your heart and mind with the creative wonders of God, and you will find millions of excellent ways to express yourself.

DIVINE PROMISE

WE ARE GOD'S MASTERPIECE. HE HAS CREATED US ANEW IN CHRIST JESUS, SO WE CAN DO THE GOOD THINGS HE PLANNED FOR US LONG AGO. *Ephesians 2:10*

Crisis

MY QUESTION *for* GOD

If I'm obeying God, why am I facing a crisis?

A MOMENT *with* GOD

One day Jesus said to his disciples, "Let's cross to the
other side of the lake." So they got into a boat and
started out. As they sailed across, Jesus settled down
for a nap. But soon a fierce storm came down on the
lake. The boat was filling with water, and they were
in real danger. The disciples went and woke him up,
shouting, "Master, Master, we're going to drown!"
When Jesus woke up, he rebuked the wind and the
raging waves. Suddenly the storm stopped and all was
calm. Then he asked them, "Where is your faith?"

LUKE 8:22-25

When Jesus heard [the young man's] answer, he
said, "There is still one thing you haven't done. Sell
all your possessions and give the money to the poor,
and you will have treasure in heaven. Then come,
follow me." But when the man heard this he became
very sad, for he was very rich. When Jesus saw this,
he said, "How hard it is for the rich to enter the
Kingdom of God! In fact, it is easier for a camel to go
through the eye of a needle than for a rich person to
enter the Kingdom of God!"   LUKE 18:22-25

The disciples were devoted followers of Jesus. They
might have thought that being involved in God's work

excluded them from the trials of life and seemed surprised when a dangerous storm threatened their lives. Yet they still knew where to turn for help. Doing the will of God does not exclude you from this world's trials. Even the most spiritually hardy face crises that shake them to the core. When you experience these, call out to Jesus for care and protection. Although the raging storm didn't awaken Jesus, the disciples' cries of need aroused him immediately. Like a mother or father who can hear their child's cry over the din of a crowd, Jesus hears you. Jesus was weary at times during his earthly life, but he is tireless as he cares for you now. When you call out to God, it is God's presence with you that breaks through your fears and calms your heart, even when the storms of life continue to rage around you.

DIVINE PROMISE

CALL ON ME WHEN YOU ARE IN TROUBLE,
AND I WILL RESCUE YOU, AND YOU WILL GIVE
ME GLORY.   *Psalm 50:15*

Criticism

MY QUESTION *for* GOD

Can I really learn anything by listening to criticism?

A MOMENT *with* GOD

Fools think their own way is right, but the wise listen to others. A fool is quick-tempered, but a wise person stays calm when insulted. An honest witness tells the truth; a false witness tells lies. Some people make cutting remarks, but the words of the wise bring healing.   PROVERBS 12:15-18

Timely advice is lovely, like golden apples in a silver basket. To one who listens, valid criticism is like a gold earring or other gold jewelry.   PROVERBS 25:11-12

*R*ejecting correction is the hallmark of a fool, but a core attribute of wisdom is a teachable heart. God has given you the gift of others' input to keep you from pursuing the wrong path. It is easy to dismiss criticism and decide you're on the right path. Sometimes it's painful to hear the truth, but it's worse to continue harmful behavior. The gentle rebuke of a trusted friend can be God's way of getting your attention. Sometimes God's guiding voice can be heard in the advice of godly people. If you're listening for God, he will always help you discern wise correction. But don't let your wounded pride make you reject constructive criticism that will help you grow.

DIVINE PROMISE

BE JOYFUL. GROW TO MATURITY. ENCOURAGE EACH OTHER. . . . THEN THE GOD OF LOVE AND PEACE WILL BE WITH YOU. *2 Corinthians 13:11*

Decisions

MY QUESTION *for* GOD

Does each decision I make really matter all that much?

A MOMENT *with* GOD

My steps have stayed on your path; I have not wavered
from following you.   PSALM 17:5

Commit your actions to the LORD, and your plans
will succeed.   PROVERBS 16:3

Oh, that we might know the LORD! Let us press on
to know him. He will respond to us as surely as the
arrival of dawn or the coming of rains in early spring.

HOSEA 6:3

*M*aking right decisions is like hiking; each step puts
you a little farther down the path. Sometimes the right
decision is simply being faithful in little things. God's
will for you today is to obey him, serve others, read his
Word, and do what is right. If you stay in the center of
his will today, you can be sure that you will be in the
center of his will twenty years from now. When you
have been faithful over time, there will come a point
where it feels that God is letting you choose which way
to go. What is really happening is that you are close
enough to God to recognize his leading in your life.

DIVINE PROMISE

SEEK HIS WILL IN ALL YOU DO, AND HE WILL
SHOW YOU WHICH PATH TO TAKE.   *Proverbs 3:6*

Deliverance

MY QUESTION *for* GOD

What are ways I can experience God's deliverance?

A MOMENT *with* GOD

[Jesus said,] "The Spirit of the LORD is upon me,
for he has anointed me to bring Good News to the
poor. He has sent me to proclaim that captives will be
released, that the blind will see, that the oppressed
will be set free, and that the time of the LORD's favor
has come."   LUKE 4:18-19

*J*esus came to deliver people who were oppressed by
the world or the powers of evil. We see this in the Gos-
pels as he delivered people from spiritual oppression
by demons. He delivered them from physical oppression by healing their diseases. He delivered them from
intellectual oppression by exposing lies and teaching
the truth that sets us free. And he spoke boldly against
the injustice of abusive leadership, especially against
religious leaders. This is why salvation is also called
deliverance. Jesus can deliver you not only from the
consequences of your sins but also from the forces in
this world that oppress you.

DIVINE PROMISE

[JESUS SAID,] "I HAVE TOLD YOU ALL THIS SO THAT YOU MAY HAVE PEACE IN ME. HERE ON EARTH YOU WILL HAVE MANY TRIALS AND SORROWS. BUT TAKE HEART, BECAUSE I HAVE OVERCOME THE WORLD." *John 16:33*

Denial

MY QUESTION *for* GOD

I thought denial was not a good thing. What kind of denial does God call me to?

A MOMENT *with* GOD

You cannot become my disciple without giving up everything you own.   LUKE 14:33

Those who belong to Christ Jesus have nailed the passions and desires of their sinful nature to his cross and crucified them there.   GALATIANS 5:24

Everything else is worthless when compared with the infinite value of knowing Christ Jesus my Lord. For his sake I have discarded everything else, counting it all as garbage, so that I could gain Christ and become one with him.   PHILIPPIANS 3:8-9

God calls you to exercise restraint and self-discipline in the way you live. This means you must deny any self-centered attitudes for the sake of obeying him. You must give up some things in order to prevent you from giving up on God. If asked, would you be willing to give up everything for God? He probably won't ask you to do something that dramatic, but he loves that kind of willing attitude in his followers.

DIVINE PROMISE

NO ONE CAN SERVE TWO MASTERS. FOR YOU WILL HATE ONE AND LOVE THE OTHER; YOU WILL BE DEVOTED TO ONE AND DESPISE THE OTHER. YOU CANNOT SERVE BOTH GOD AND MONEY. THAT IS WHY I TELL YOU NOT TO WORRY ABOUT EVERYDAY LIFE—WHETHER YOU HAVE ENOUGH FOOD AND DRINK, OR ENOUGH CLOTHES TO WEAR. ISN'T LIFE MORE THAN FOOD, AND YOUR BODY MORE THAN CLOTHING?   *Matthew 6:24-25*

Dependence

MY QUESTION *for* GOD

How does dependence on God make me stronger?

A MOMENT *with* GOD

I know the LORD is always with me. I will not be shaken, for he is right beside me.   PSALM 16:8

[Jesus said,] "I am with you always, even to the end of the age."   MATTHEW 28:20

Humble yourselves before the Lord, and he will lift
you up in honor.   JAMES 4:10

*Y*ou're never alone when you belong to God, for his
Spirit is always with you. And there is no one more dependable than the One who created you and knows you
better than anyone else does. One of the mysteries of the
Christian faith is that the more you humble yourself and
depend on God, the stronger you become in character
and integrity. When you are completely dependent on
God, you can rely completely on his strength.

DIVINE PROMISE

DO NOT BE AFRAID, FOR I AM WITH YOU.
Isaiah 43:5

Depression

MY QUESTION *for* GOD

*Where can I find inspiration and encouragement in times
of depression?*

A MOMENT *with* GOD

Even in darkness I cannot hide from you.   PSALM 139:12

Jesus said, "Come to me, all of you who are weary
and carry heavy burdens, and I will give you rest."

MATTHEW 11:28

No power in the sky above or in the earth below—
indeed, nothing in all creation will ever be able to
separate us from the love of God that is revealed in
Christ Jesus our Lord.

ROMANS 8:39

*S*ooner or later most of us experience some form of
depression. It can descend slowly and hang in the air
like an all-day rain. It can overwhelm like an avalanche
of darkness. It can be the result of a specific experience
of failure or loss, or it can invade your mind for no
discernable reason. No matter how low you get, there
is no depth to which you can descend that God is not
present with you. Even if you don't feel his presence, he
has not abandoned you. God can use your depression to
get you to slow down and rest long enough to be with
him. As you meet with him in prayer and with an open
Bible, you welcome the Holy Spirit to do his work of
comfort, transformation, and encouragement—often
in ways you cannot explain. The light of God's com-
forting presence can drive the darkness of depression
from your soul.

DIVINE PROMISE
HE LIFTED ME OUT OF THE PIT OF DESPAIR.
Psalm 40:2

Desires

MY QUESTION *for* GOD

How can I know if my own desires match God's desires for me?

A MOMENT *with* GOD

[David] sent someone to find out who she was, and he was told, "She is Bathsheba, the daughter of Eliam and the wife of Uriah the Hittite." Then David sent messengers to get her.   2 SAMUEL 11:3-4

Fix your thoughts on what is true, and honorable, and right, and pure, and lovely, and admirable.

PHILIPPIANS 4:8

David's selfish desires overpowered his reason. His desire for Bathsheba caused him to commit adultery and to have her husband murdered, which resulted in much grief for his family. When you are wondering whether what you desire is right or wrong, consider the long-term consequences. Is the object of your desire good, consistent with God's Word, and harmless to others? When you've answered that question, you'll know which choice to make.

DIVINE PROMISE

IF YOU ARE WISE AND UNDERSTAND GOD'S WAYS, PROVE IT BY LIVING AN HONORABLE LIFE, DOING GOOD WORKS WITH THE HUMILITY THAT COMES FROM WISDOM. *James 3:13*

Desirability

MY QUESTION *for* GOD

How am I desirable to God?

A MOMENT *with* GOD

My heart has heard you say, "Come and talk with me." And my heart responds, "LORD, I am coming."

PSALM 27:8

He loves us with unfailing love; the LORD's faithfulness endures forever. Praise the LORD!

PSALM 117:2

See how very much our Father loves us, for he calls us his children.

1 JOHN 3:1

Your very existence is proof of God's faithful love for you. You are not a creature randomly evolved from a prehistoric primordial soup. God created you in his own image to have a relationship with him. He made you and equipped you with certain abilities to use for his special purposes. When you ignore or shrug off how God made you, you miss out on experiencing the kinds of service and abilities that make you a desirable woman of God.

DIVINE PROMISE

I AM WRITING TO ALL OF YOU IN ROME WHO ARE LOVED BY GOD AND ARE CALLED TO BE HIS OWN HOLY PEOPLE. MAY GOD OUR FATHER

AND THE LORD JESUS CHRIST GIVE YOU GRACE
AND PEACE.   *Romans 1:7*

Differences

MY QUESTION *for* GOD

How do our differences help us to accomplish more for God?

A MOMENT *with* GOD

God called the light "day" and the darkness "night."
And evening passed and morning came, marking the
first day.   GENESIS 1:5

People often say about each other, "We're as different
as night and day." Have you ever thought about how
that might be a good thing? God, in his infinite
wisdom, made light and darkness work together
to form one day. Both are necessary because each
facilitates life in a different way. Just as light and
dark are different but united, you can be united
with people who are different from you by using
your differences to accomplish something whole.
Employing your differences to accomplish something
significant is a wonderful picture of harmony.

In that day the wolf and the lamb will live
together; the leopard will lie down with the baby
goat. The calf and the yearling will be safe with the
lion, and a little child will lead them all. The cow
will graze near the bear. The cub and the calf will lie
down together. The lion will eat hay like a cow.

                                                    ISAIAH 11:6-7

"The wolf and the lamb will feed together. The lion will eat hay like a cow. But the snakes will eat dust. In those days no one will be hurt or destroyed on my holy mountain. I, the LORD, have spoken!" ISAIAH 65:25

Although you may fear that you and your spouse or boss or neighbor might never be compatible, take hope in the fact that God will one day restore camaraderie even among the greatest of enemies in the animal kingdom. If God has such a wonderful plan for the animals, how much more you have to look forward to.

All of you together are Christ's body, and each of you is a part of it.   1 CORINTHIANS 12:27

He makes the whole body fit together perfectly. As each part does its own special work, it helps the other parts grow, so that the whole body is healthy and growing and full of love.   EPHESIANS 4:16

Christ designed you to contribute to the body of believers. The human body is made up of separate and different parts, yet all parts work together to sustain life. It is the same with the church, the body of believers. Each person is a separate part with a unique role to play. Your role will be different from the roles of others, but the beauty is that these differences help sustain the body of Christ and allow it to flourish. Sometimes, differences can enhance harmony.

DIVINE PROMISE

LIVE IN HARMONY AND PEACE. THEN THE GOD
OF LOVE AND PEACE WILL BE WITH YOU.

2 Corinthians 13:11

Dignity

MY QUESTION *for* GOD

Can I follow God and maintain my dignity?

A MOMENT *with* GOD

God created human beings in his own image. In the
image of God he created them; male and female he
created them.   GENESIS 1:27

You made [people] only a little lower than God and
crowned them with glory and honor.   PSALM 8:5

The LORD delights in his people; he crowns the
humble with victory.   PSALM 149:4

Dignity is the quality of worth and significance that
every human being has been given when created in the
image of God. Dignity has two angles—recognizing
your own worth before God, and recognizing that
same worth in others. Unfortunately it is human nature to rank everyone from important to insignificant.
But a proper view of dignity motivates you to see others as God sees them, worthy of your love and respect
no matter where they live or what they do. When you

behave respectably, have self-control and strong faith, and are loving and patient, you show dignity. This fosters a deep respect for others as you build them up rather than rank them as being beneath you. When you realize how God esteems you, the opinions of others matter less.

DIVINE PROMISE

CHOOSE A GOOD REPUTATION OVER GREAT RICHES; BEING HELD IN HIGH ESTEEM IS BETTER THAN SILVER OR GOLD.   *Proverbs 22:1*

Disappointment

MY QUESTION *for* GOD

How do I handle life's disappointments?

A MOMENT *with* GOD

Always continue to fear the LORD. You will be rewarded for this; your hope will not be disappointed.   PROVERBS 23:17-18

A man planted a fig tree in his garden and came again and again to see if there was any fruit on it, but he was always disappointed. Finally, he said to his gardener, "I've waited three years, and there hasn't been a single fig! Cut it down. It's just taking up space in the garden."   LUKE 13:6-7

Dear friends, don't be surprised at the fiery trials you are going through, as if something strange were happening to you.

1 PETER 4:12

*D*isappointment, in some form, probably haunts you almost every day. Perhaps you didn't get everything done, someone hurt you or let you down, you let someone else down, or things just didn't go your way. You may have experienced that awful feeling of not being "good enough." When disappointment comes, you might ask "what if" questions that lead to regret, or play the blame game so that someone else is at fault. Neither of these responses is appropriate, and both can lead to discouragement, depression, anger, shame, or bitterness. When disappointment dominates your thoughts, you can end up a negative, sad, grumpy person. But if you see disappointment as an opportunity to learn and grow, or if you choose to focus on what you have and not on what you've missed, you can view disappointment from the proper perspective. Life is full of disappointment. But God wants you to dwell on what can be, not on what could have been. The next time you feel disappointed, remember all you have, determine to grow through the experience, and be happy that you have the approval of the One who really matters.

DIVINE PROMISE

THIS HOPE WILL NOT LEAD TO
DISAPPOINTMENT. FOR WE KNOW HOW
DEARLY GOD LOVES US, BECAUSE HE HAS GIVEN

US THE HOLY SPIRIT TO FILL OUR HEARTS WITH
HIS LOVE. *Romans 5:5*

Disapproval

My Question *for* God

*How can I befriend others when I disapprove of their
immoral lifestyle?*

A Moment *with* God

When Jesus came by, he looked up at Zacchaeus and
called him by name. "Zacchaeus!" he said. "Quick,
come down! I must be a guest in your home today."
Zacchaeus quickly climbed down and took Jesus
to his house in great excitement and joy. But the
people were displeased. "He has gone to be the guest
of a notorious sinner," they grumbled. . . . Jesus
responded, ". . . The Son of Man came to seek and
save those who are lost." Luke 19:5-7, 9-10

∞

$\mathcal{I}$f you picture Jesus enjoying the company of only
good, churchgoing people and being too holy to hang
out with immoral people, you are mistaken. Jesus focused on finding those who were farthest from him and
ministering to their needs. Following Jesus' example
means looking past people's behavior to their soul. It
takes special effort to love those you disapprove of, but
they are the people who most need a godly friend. Your
knowledge of God's ways shouldn't separate you from

the ungodly; rather, it qualifies you to reach them and
serve them in love.

DIVINE PROMISE

EVEN THE SON OF MAN CAME NOT TO BE
SERVED BUT TO SERVE OTHERS AND TO GIVE
HIS LIFE AS A RANSOM FOR MANY.   *Matthew 20:28*

Distractions

MY QUESTION *for* GOD

How can I serve God when my life is full of distractions?

A MOMENT *with* GOD

The jailer called for lights and ran to the dungeon and
fell down trembling before Paul and Silas. Then he
brought them out and asked, "Sirs, what must I do to
be saved?" They replied, "Believe in the Lord Jesus
and you will be saved, along with everyone in your
household." And they shared the word of the Lord
with him.   ACTS 16:29-32

*M*ost people would look at a jail sentence as a defi-
nite distraction from their ability to serve God. Not
Paul and Silas! Their location didn't keep them from
their mission. They had been involved in a great ministry around the world; now they were confined to a
small room with a very small audience. God seemed

to be just fine with that. Instead of pushing away the distraction, Paul and Silas embraced it! Sometimes a distraction seems as restricting as a jail cell. But maybe God wants you to focus for a while on who and what are right in front of you. What you see as a distraction may actually be a calling from God to minister to new people in a new place.

DIVINE PROMISE

ACCEPT THE WAY GOD DOES THINGS,
FOR WHO CAN STRAIGHTEN WHAT HE HAS
MADE CROOKED?   *Ecclesiastes 7:13*

Doubt

MY QUESTION *for* GOD

Can God use me, even when I doubt myself?

A MOMENT *with* GOD

Moses pleaded with the LORD, "O Lord, I'm not very good with words. I never have been, and I'm not now, even though you have spoken to me. I get tongue-tied, and my words get tangled." Then the LORD asked Moses, "Who makes a person's mouth? Who decides whether people speak or do not speak, hear or do not hear, see or do not see? Is it not I, the LORD? Now go! I will be with you as you speak, and I will instruct you in what to say." But Moses again pleaded, "Lord, please! Send anyone else."   EXODUS 4:10-13

*M*oses was certain he could not do what God was asking of him. The task was too big, and Moses was scared, unprepared, and full of doubt. But in some ways this was Moses' greatest asset. God works through humble hearts that depend on him. Moses had a realistic picture of his abilities. He knew he couldn't do the job by his own power or skill, so he had two choices: walk away, or let God work through him. Fortunately, he chose wisely. When the task ahead of you seems too big, when you doubt your ability to see it through but know God wants you to do it, that is the time to trust him to work through you.

DIVINE PROMISE

IS ANYTHING TOO HARD FOR THE LORD?
I WILL RETURN ABOUT THIS TIME NEXT YEAR,
AND SARAH WILL HAVE A SON. *Genesis 18:14*

Doubt

MY QUESTION *for* GOD

How does overcoming doubt strengthen my faith?

A MOMENT *with* GOD

The LORD said to Gideon, "You have too many warriors with you. If I let all of you fight the Midianites, the Israelites will boast to me that they saved themselves by their own strength. Therefore, tell the people, 'Whoever is timid or afraid may leave this mountain and go home.'" So 22,000 of them went home, leaving only 10,000 who were willing to fight. But the LORD told Gideon, "There are still too many! Bring them down to the spring, and I will test them to determine who will go with you and who will not."

JUDGES 7:2-4

*D*oubt can be a trapdoor to fear, or it can be a doorway to confident faith. When you doubt God's ability to help you in the face of great odds but you trust him anyway and he acts, your faith is strengthened. God wants you to express your faith in him *before* he acts. So when God calls you to a task, as he did with Gideon, don't be surprised if at first it seems the obstacles are stacking up. This may be a test of your faith; God may be preparing to deepen your faith and strengthen your character so that you know it is really God—rather than your own efforts—who is coming to your rescue. As Gideon's army dwindled, he realized he was no longer in charge. Only God could help him now. When you realize that you can't accomplish the job on your own, are ready to give God the credit rather than take it for yourself, and courageously hold on to your faith that God has called you to do something for him, then you are in a position to see God work.

DIVINE PROMISE

WHEN DOUBTS FILLED MY MIND, YOUR
COMFORT GAVE ME RENEWED HOPE
AND CHEER. *Psalm 94:19*

Dreams

MY QUESTION *for* GOD

Does God still speak through dreams today?

A MOMENT *with* GOD

Long ago God spoke many times and in many ways
to our ancestors through the prophets. And now in
these final days, he has spoken to us through his Son.

HEBREWS 1:1-2

In the Old Testament, God often spoke to his prophets in dreams or visions. These dreams often revealed
something about the future in order to verify the trustworthiness of God—that he would do what he had
promised to do. These dreams were confirmed when
the real event happened. This verse, however, seems
to be saying that since the earthly ministry of Jesus,
dreams may not be as necessary, because God has revealed himself and his plans more clearly through his
Son. When Jesus ascended into heaven, he left behind
his Holy Spirit to give wisdom and discernment. In
addition, God's Word is available to more people than
ever. This does not mean that God no longer speaks
through dreams or visions, but he wants you to regularly read his Word, communicate directly with Jesus,
and rely on the Holy Spirit to know his will. The key is
to have a heart that is ready to receive God's guidance
and is open and ready to hear from him at all times and
in all ways.

DIVINE PROMISE

THE WORD BECAME HUMAN AND MADE HIS
HOME AMONG US. HE WAS FULL OF UNFAILING
LOVE AND FAITHFULNESS. AND WE HAVE SEEN
HIS GLORY, THE GLORY OF THE FATHER'S ONE
AND ONLY SON.   *John 1:14*

Emotions

MY QUESTION *for* GOD

How does the power of God help me to control my emotions?

A MOMENT *with* GOD

Guard your heart above all else, for it determines the
course of your life.   PROVERBS 4:23

I will give you a new heart, and I will put a new spirit
in you.   EZEKIEL 36:26

Let the Spirit renew your thoughts and attitudes.

EPHESIANS 4:23

Emotions are a good gift from God. They are evidence
that you are made in God's image, for the Bible shows
God displaying the whole range of emotions from anger to zeal. But like any gift from God, emotions can
be misused. Instead of a blessing, they can become a
curse. Emotions come from the heart, where there
is a desperate battle going on between your old and
new natures. Your heart gets caught in a tug-of-war

between your emotions. Your new nature helps you use your emotions to reflect his character, which will help you love people in healthy ways. Your sinful nature, however, tries to get you to redirect and lose control of your emotions so that you lapse into behavior that is harmful to yourself and others. Emotions gone bad tempt you to impulsively seek the pleasures of sin. For example, the same emotion—love—can be a powerful force for good when it cares for someone in need. But it can be a powerful force for evil if it is allowed to turn into lust or jealous rage. Learn to understand your emotions and direct them in ways that are productive, not destructive. The issue isn't the power or intensity of the emotion, but what it leads you to do.

DIVINE PROMISE

THE HOLY SPIRIT PRODUCES THIS KIND
OF FRUIT IN OUR LIVES: LOVE, JOY,
PEACE, PATIENCE, KINDNESS, GOODNESS,
FAITHFULNESS, GENTLENESS, AND
SELF-CONTROL.   *Galatians 5:22-23*

Empathy

MY QUESTION *for* GOD

How does empathy nurture genuine love?

A Moment *with* God

Be happy with those who are happy, and weep with
those who weep.   ROMANS 12:15

I have the daily burden of my concern for all the
churches. Who is weak without my feeling that
weakness? Who is led astray, and I do not burn
with anger?   2 CORINTHIANS 11:28-29

*E*mpathy is more than feeling bad for someone who
is going through a hard time. It is more than feeling
glad for someone who has had success. Empathy is allowing yourself to feel the same emotions that other
people feel—like crawling inside them to experience
their pain or joy. Empathy leaves no room for jealousy
over a friend's success and no room to enjoy the failure
of an enemy. As you empathize with others, God can
break through to your own heart, softening it toward
others and helping you to know exactly how to comfort
and support them and meet their needs. As you seek to
understand others, you will grow in your knowledge of
how to best show love to them in obedience to God's
commandment to love one another.

DIVINE PROMISE

IF ONE PART SUFFERS, ALL THE PARTS SUFFER
WITH IT, AND IF ONE PART IS HONORED, ALL
THE PARTS ARE GLAD.   *1 Corinthians 12:26*

Emptiness

MY QUESTIONS *for* GOD

Why does life sometimes seem so empty? How do I fill the emptiness inside me?

A MOMENT *with* GOD

Let them no longer fool themselves by trusting in empty riches, for emptiness will be their only reward.   JOB 15:31

[Jesus said,] "When an evil spirit leaves a person, it goes into the desert, searching for rest. But when it finds none, it says, 'I will return to the person I came from.' So it returns and finds that its former home is all swept and in order. Then the spirit finds seven other spirits more evil than itself, and they all enter the person and live there. And so that person is worse off than before."   LUKE 11:24-26

Jesus replied, "Anyone who drinks this water will soon become thirsty again. But those who drink the water I give will never be thirsty again. It becomes a fresh, bubbling spring within them, giving them eternal life."   JOHN 4:13-14

A woman's car coughs, sputters, and finally stops, miles from town—her gas tank is empty. A hiker, far from camp, swallows the last few drops of water from his canteen—there is nothing left. A husband buries his young wife, wondering how he can go on, how he can raise his little children by himself—his heart feels empty. When something is empty—a gas tank, canteen, printer cartridge, cereal box—it's either not going to work or it's not going to satisfy. But when some*one* is empty, motivation, meaning, and purpose are lost. There seems no reason to go on. Many things can cause you to feel empty—the death of a loved one, the end of a friendship, being ignored or rejected. These empty feelings all have one thing in common: some kind of loss. Loss empties your emotional tank. Your reserves are used up, and now you're hungry and thirsty for something to fill and satisfy. This is the moment Satan's been waiting for. He is always ready to move into an empty heart, to deceive you into thinking that what he offers can satisfy. But when your heart is filled with the love, truth, and goodness of God through the presence of the Holy Spirit, there is little room for evil to enter. It is only when you are filled with God's Spirit that meaning, purpose, and satisfaction are restored.

DIVINE PROMISE

I PRAY THAT GOD, THE SOURCE OF HOPE, WILL FILL YOU COMPLETELY WITH JOY AND PEACE BECAUSE YOU TRUST IN HIM. THEN YOU WILL OVERFLOW WITH CONFIDENT HOPE THROUGH THE POWER OF THE HOLY SPIRIT. *Romans 15:13*

Encouragement

How does God's gift of encouragement renew my life?

A MOMENT *with* GOD

After the death of Moses the LORD's servant, the LORD spoke to Joshua son of Nun, Moses' assistant. He said, "Moses my servant is dead. Therefore, the time has come for you to lead these people, the Israelites, across the Jordan River into the land I am giving them. I promise you what I promised Moses: 'Wherever you set foot, you will be on land I have given you—from the Negev wilderness in the south to the Lebanon mountains in the north, from the Euphrates River in the east to the Mediterranean Sea in the west, including all the land of the Hittites.' No one will be able to stand against you as long as you live. For I will be with you as I was with Moses. I will not fail you or abandon you."   JOSHUA 1:1-5

*J*oshua's strength and resolve may have weakened over the daunting task of leading all the Israelites into a land of giants. So God prepared him—and the rest of the people—with specific words of encouragement. At times you may long for someone to come beside you to lift you up and strengthen you. How much better if that someone were God himself! The word *courage* is embedded in the word *encouragement*. Encouragement gives you the courage to go on, to renew your commitment and resolve. It inspires you with hope that

your task is not in vain—that you can make a difference. God's encouragement is a beautiful spiritual gift
that gives you a renewed desire and commitment to
obey him. Like Joshua, you find courage not by looking within or by looking at your circumstances, but by
looking up to the sovereign God.

DIVINE PROMISE

BE STRONG AND COURAGEOUS! DO NOT BE
AFRAID OR DISCOURAGED. FOR THE LORD
YOUR GOD IS WITH YOU WHEREVER YOU GO.
Joshua 1:9

Endurance

MY QUESTION *for* GOD

How can I be effective in serving Christ over the long haul?

A MOMENT *with* GOD

"Are you seeking great things for yourself? Don't do
it! I will bring great disaster upon all these people;
but I will give you your life as a reward wherever you
go. I, the LORD, have spoken!"   JEREMIAH 45:5

The greatest among you must be a servant.

MATTHEW 23:11

$\mathcal{I}$t is certainly difficult to do good over a long period of time when life throws you so many trials and temptations. An enduring faith, however, is up to the challenge. The ability to be steady in goodness is born out of godly motives. The desire for status, control, or acceptance is not an adequate motive for long-term discipleship. You will inevitably be disappointed, for Jesus promises you none of these. In fact, Jesus taught that to be the greatest, you must be willing to be the least. Serve because you love him and because you love others in his name. This will not make ministry easy, but it will enable you to endure as you find deep joy in serving others.

DIVINE PROMISE

LET'S NOT GET TIRED OF DOING WHAT IS GOOD. AT JUST THE RIGHT TIME WE WILL REAP A HARVEST OF BLESSING IF WE DON'T GIVE UP.
Galatians 6:9

Energy

MY QUESTION *for* GOD

How can I find more energy?

A MOMENT *with* GOD

Work with enthusiasm, as though you were working for the Lord rather than for people.   EPHESIANS 6:7

When you do your work as if you were doing it for
God, you can work with more enthusiasm and energy
because your tasks are infused with a sense of divine
purpose. Doing work for God means working to
please him, not just to get through the task. Trying to
imitate the way he would do your work helps you to
see how you can influence those around you.

Dear brothers and sisters, I have not achieved it,
but I focus on this one thing: Forgetting the past and
looking forward to what lies ahead.   PHILIPPIANS 3:13

You will have more energy for today and tomorrow
if you don't waste energy focusing on the past. The
more you drag around from your past, the heavier
the load you will carry today and the less energy you
will have for tomorrow. God's Word tells you to free
yourself from the past and funnel your energy into
making today and tomorrow all you want them to be.

No discipline is enjoyable while it is happening—
it's painful! But afterward there will be a peaceful
harvest of right living for those who are trained in
this way. So take a new grip with your tired hands
and strengthen your weak knees.   HEBREWS 12:11-12

When you know you are doing the right thing, it can
rejuvenate you because you realize that God is pleased
with your actions. God's approval stimulates greater
obedience.

DIVINE PROMISE

MY HEALTH MAY FAIL, AND MY SPIRIT MAY
GROW WEAK, BUT GOD REMAINS THE
STRENGTH OF MY HEART; HE IS MINE FOREVER.

Psalm 73:26

Eternity

MY QUESTION *for* GOD

What is eternal life going to be like?

A MOMENT *with* GOD

No eye has seen, no ear has heard, and no mind
has imagined what God has prepared for those who
love him.   1 CORINTHIANS 2:9

We know that when this earthly tent we live in is
taken down (that is, when we die and leave this
earthly body), we will have a house in heaven, an
eternal body made for us by God himself and not by
human hands.   2 CORINTHIANS 5:1

Look, God's home is now among his people! He
will live with them, and they will be his people.
God himself will be with them. He will wipe every
tear from their eyes, and there will be no more death
or sorrow or crying or pain. All these things are
gone forever.   REVELATION 21:3-4

𝓔ternity is not merely an extension of your life here on earth, where you suffer, grieve, and hurt. God promises something new. He will restore this earth to the way he once created it—a beautiful place with no sin, sorrow, or pain. You will live in the world you long for without evil and suffering. God created humans for this earth, so the new earth will have a lot of similarities to this one, but it will be better and more amazing in every way. You will be in God's presence and forever filled with joy. You don't have to worry about sitting around on some cloud and strumming a harp. Eternity will have plenty of fun, fulfilling, and purposeful things to do.

DIVINE PROMISE

[JESUS SAID,] "I TELL YOU THE TRUTH, ANYONE WHO BELIEVES HAS ETERNAL LIFE." *John 6:47*

𝓔vil

MY QUESTION *for* GOD

If God is good, why does he let people do evil things?

A MOMENT *with* GOD

The LORD God placed the man in the Garden of Eden to tend and watch over it. But the LORD God warned him, "You may freely eat the fruit of every tree in the garden—except the tree of the knowledge of good and evil. If you eat its fruit, you are sure to die."

GENESIS 2:15-17

I went into your sanctuary, O God, and I finally
understood the destiny of the wicked. Truly, you
put them on a slippery path and send them sliding
over the cliff to destruction. In an instant they are
destroyed, completely swept away by terrors. When
you arise, O Lord, you will laugh at their silly ideas as
a person laughs at dreams in the morning.

PSALM 73:17-20

Stay alert! Watch out for your great enemy, the devil.
He prowls around like a roaring lion, looking for
someone to devour. Stand firm against him, and be
strong in your faith.   1 PETER 5:8-9

Genuine love requires the freedom to choose. From
the beginning, God desired a loving relationship with
you, so he gave you this freedom. But with ability to
make choices comes the possibility of choosing your
own way over God's way. Your own way always leads
to sin, because all people are born with a sinful nature
(see Romans 3:23). This breaks God's heart, but the
alternative would have been for him to make us robots,
not humans. Evil still exists, and evil people continue
to do evil things, but you can choose to do what is
right. When you do so, God is pleased, good prevails,
and Satan loses ground. Eventually, God will destroy
the power of evil for all time. Until that day, you can
fight evil by choosing to obey God and do good.

DIVINE PROMISE

DON'T LET ANYONE CAPTURE YOU WITH
EMPTY PHILOSOPHIES AND HIGH-SOUNDING
NONSENSE THAT COME FROM HUMAN
THINKING AND FROM THE SPIRITUAL POWERS
OF THIS WORLD, RATHER THAN FROM CHRIST.

Colossians 2:8

Experience

MY QUESTION *for* GOD

How can God use my limited experience?

A MOMENT *with* GOD

[God] chose his servant David, calling him from
the sheep pens. He took David from tending the
ewes and lambs and made him the shepherd of
Jacob's descendants—God's own people, Israel. He
cared for them with a true heart and led them with
skillful hands.   PSALM 78:70-72

Do the best you can wherever you are—and remember that God wastes nothing. Instead, he uses everything to further his purposes. David's first job was
shepherding—hardly the recommended grooming for
a future monarch! Yet the lessons David learned on
the hills with the sheep served him well on the throne,
so much so that he ruled not as a tyrant but as a shepherd. God will use you in whatever situation you find

yourself, and he will use your circumstances to prepare
you for future service. God's plan is unfolding now,
not just later in the future. Your greatest success will
come from your obedience to God as he carries out his
plans through you. God will make use of your training
and your experience to make you even more fruitful
for him.

DIVINE PROMISE

[JESUS SAID,] "YOU DIDN'T CHOOSE ME. I CHOSE
YOU. I APPOINTED YOU TO GO AND PRODUCE
LASTING FRUIT, SO THAT THE FATHER WILL
GIVE YOU WHATEVER YOU ASK FOR, USING
MY NAME."   *John 15:16*

Failure

MY QUESTION *for* GOD

What is failure in God's eyes?

A MOMENT *with* GOD

It's your sins that have cut you off from God. Because
of your sins, he has turned away and will not listen
anymore.   ISAIAH 59:2

[Jesus said,] "Anyone who listens to my teaching and
follows it is wise, like a person who builds a house
on solid rock. Though the rain comes in torrents and
the floodwaters rise and the winds beat against that

house, it won't collapse because it is built on bedrock.
But anyone who hears my teaching and doesn't
obey it is foolish, like a person who builds a house
on sand. When the rains and floods come and the
winds beat against that house, it will collapse with a
mighty crash."   MATTHEW 7:24-27

What do you benefit if you gain the whole world but
lose your own soul? Is anything worth more than
your soul?   MATTHEW 16:26

If you managed a successful business, raised a good
family, won all kinds of community awards, and re-
tired comfortably, would you say that your life had
been a success? God says you would have failed if you
had done all of these things apart from him. Life apart
from God now means life apart from him for eternity.
Failure in God's eyes is not living the way he created
you to live. God instructs you to live a certain way for
a very good reason: to help you make the most of life
both now and forever. Sin results in failure because it is
living contrary to God's perfect plan for you. God gave
you the gift of life and created you for relationship with
him. Your greatest failure would be to reject that way
of life and to reject the God who gave you life. Don't
fail by neglecting or ignoring him.

DIVINE PROMISE
THE LORD DIRECTS THE STEPS OF THE GODLY.
HE DELIGHTS IN EVERY DETAIL OF THEIR

LIVES. THOUGH THEY STUMBLE, THEY WILL
NEVER FALL, FOR THE LORD HOLDS THEM BY
THE HAND. *Psalm 37:23-24*

MY QUESTION *for* GOD

How does God strengthen my faith, even when I can't see him?

A MOMENT *with* GOD

Elisha prayed, "O LORD, open his eyes and let him
see!" The LORD opened the young man's eyes, and
when he looked up, he saw that the hillside around
Elisha was filled with horses and chariots of fire.

2 KINGS 6:17

[Jesus] said to Thomas, "Put your finger here, and
look at my hands. Put your hand into the wound in
my side. Don't be faithless any longer. Believe!" "My
Lord and my God!" Thomas exclaimed. Then Jesus
told him, "You believe because you have seen me.
Blessed are those who believe without seeing me."

JOHN 20:27-29

Faith comes from hearing, that is, hearing the Good
News about Christ.   ROMANS 10:17

The people's minds were hardened, and to this day
whenever the old covenant is being read, the same
veil covers their minds so they cannot understand the

truth. And this veil can be removed only by believing
in Christ.   2 CORINTHIANS 3:14

𝓕aith is not simply a matter of positive thinking or
human effort. Faith is divinely inspired by the Holy
Spirit working through the Word of God. Your faith
grows as you read the stories of God's work through
people across the centuries and you realize he will do
the same in you. The strongest faith is not one based
on physical senses but on spiritual conviction. There is
a spiritual element to this world that you cannot see,
but it is very real. Your faith will become stronger the
more you ask God to sharpen your "spiritual vision," so
that you can sense and see the results of God's work in
your life and in the lives of those around you.

DIVINE PROMISE

FAITH IS THE CONFIDENCE THAT WHAT WE
HOPE FOR WILL ACTUALLY HAPPEN.   *Hebrews 11:1*

𝓕aithfulness

MY QUESTION *for* GOD

What impact does my faithfulness to God have on others?

A MOMENT *with* GOD

Joseph assigned the best land of Egypt—the region
of Rameses—to his father and his brothers, and he

settled them there, just as Pharaoh had commanded. And Joseph provided food for his father and his brothers in amounts appropriate to the number of their dependents, including the smallest children.

GENESIS 47:11-12

Each generation tells of your faithfulness to the next.

ISAIAH 38:19

𝓘t is both the privilege and obligation of each generation to reveal to the next the faithfulness of God. God honored Joseph's faithfulness by blessing him and his family. God's blessings for your faithfulness often overflow to those around you. Likewise, you are often the benefactor of other people's faithfulness to God. You can leave a rich heritage by building this awareness into the minds of your children and grandchildren. When the words and actions of your life "sing a duet" of faithfulness to God, you give your children an example of faithfulness to treasure throughout their lifetimes. This is of far more lasting value than any other kind of inheritance we might leave behind.

DIVINE PROMISE

THE LOVE OF THE LORD REMAINS FOREVER
WITH THOSE WHO FEAR HIM. HIS SALVATION
EXTENDS TO THE CHILDREN'S CHILDREN OF
THOSE WHO ARE FAITHFUL TO HIS COVENANT,
OF THOSE WHO OBEY HIS COMMANDMENTS!
Psalm 103:17-18

Family

MY QUESTION *for* GOD

Can my family make a difference?

A MOMENT *with* GOD

[God said,] "My Spirit will not leave them, and neither will these words I have given you. They will be on your lips and on the lips of your children and your children's children forever."   ISAIAH 59:21

Peter replied, "Each of you must repent of your sins and turn to God, and be baptized in the name of Jesus Christ for the forgiveness of your sins. Then you will receive the gift of the Holy Spirit."   ACTS 2:38

*T*oo often we think about our impact in individualistic terms. How can *I* make an impact? What can *I* do? But God works through groups of people too, especially families, because a group of people passionate about God can really make an enormous impact. How can your family be influential for God? Start by praying, not just for the individuals in your family but also for your family as a whole, knowing that God wants to use you to accomplish great things for him. You never know how your family could have a profound impact on another's life.

DIVINE PROMISE

HOW JOYFUL ARE THOSE WHO FEAR THE LORD
AND DELIGHT IN OBEYING HIS COMMANDS.
THEIR CHILDREN WILL BE SUCCESSFUL
EVERYWHERE; AN ENTIRE GENERATION OF
GODLY PEOPLE WILL BE BLESSED. *Psalm 112:1-3*

Fear

MY QUESTION *for* GOD

How does fearing God help me to conquer my other fears?

A MOMENT *with* GOD

Be strong and courageous! Do not be afraid and do
not panic before them. For the LORD your God will
personally go ahead of you. He will neither fail you
nor abandon you.   DEUTERONOMY 31:6

Let the whole world fear the LORD, and let everyone
stand in awe of him.   PSALM 33:8

God is our refuge and strength, always ready to
help in times of trouble. So we will not fear when
earthquakes come and the mountains crumble into
the sea.   PSALM 46:1-2

Think of it this way: Should you fear fire or elec-
tricity? Certainly you should always have a healthy
respect for the power they both possess. If you do,
you can enjoy the blessings of warmth and light. But

disregarding such power can bring destruction. In the same way, you fear God in the sense of respecting his power, holiness, and authority. But properly fearing God is the key to experiencing all the blessings that come from tapping into his power and having a relationship with him. When you approach him with this respect and awe, you also find that he is tender, loving, and compassionate.

DIVINE PROMISE

HOW JOYFUL ARE THOSE WHO FEAR THE LORD—ALL WHO FOLLOW HIS WAYS! *Psalm 128:1*

Following

MY QUESTION *for* GOD

Why does following God seem so hard sometimes?

A MOMENT *with* GOD

Be strong and courageous, and do the work. Don't be afraid or discouraged, for the LORD God, my God, is with you. He will not fail you or forsake you.

1 CHRONICLES 28:20

Jesus said to his disciples, "If any of you wants to be my follower, you must turn from your selfish ways, take up your cross, and follow me." MATTHEW 16:24

The fact that you are following God in something doesn't make it easy. In fact, the more important a task is, the more evil forces will throw up roadblocks. If God is leading you in a certain direction, don't give up just because the going gets tough. Keep moving forward boldly with your eyes fixed on God, and your faith will be strengthened as you obey him.

DIVINE PROMISE

WHEN TROUBLES COME YOUR WAY, CONSIDER IT AN OPPORTUNITY FOR GREAT JOY. FOR YOU KNOW THAT WHEN YOUR FAITH IS TESTED, YOUR ENDURANCE HAS A CHANCE TO GROW. SO LET IT GROW, FOR WHEN YOUR ENDURANCE IS FULLY DEVELOPED, YOU WILL BE PERFECT AND COMPLETE, NEEDING NOTHING.   *James 1:2-4*

Forgiveness

MY QUESTION *for* GOD

What is the healing power of forgiveness?

A MOMENT *with* GOD

Esau ran to meet [Jacob] and embraced him, threw his arms around his neck, and kissed him. And they both wept.   GENESIS 33:4

Jesus said, "Father, forgive them, for they don't know what they are doing."   LUKE 23:34

Forgiveness is the pathway to freedom; it is both a decision and a process. Sometimes you must *decide* to forgive before you have feelings of mercy and a desire to offer forgiveness. When you forgive someone who has wronged you, you are freed from bitterness and resentment that can saturate your soul like toxic waste. And when someone forgives you, you are free from indebtedness to that person. As you release the hurt inflicted on you, you will be healed and free to grow beyond the pain. Is there someone you need to forgive so that you can move forward?

DIVINE PROMISE

FORGIVE US OUR SINS, AS WE HAVE FORGIVEN THOSE WHO SIN AGAINST US.   *Matthew 6:12*

Freedom

MY QUESTION *for* GOD

How does the truth about Jesus allow me to experience freedom?

A MOMENT *with* GOD

Jesus said to the people who believed in him, "You are truly my disciples if you remain faithful to my teachings. And you will know the truth, and the truth will set you free."   JOHN 8:31-32

Sin is no longer your master, for you no longer live under the requirements of the law. Instead, you live under the freedom of God's grace.   ROMANS 6:14

The Scriptures declare that we are all prisoners of sin, so we receive God's promise of freedom only by believing in Jesus Christ.   GALATIANS 3:22

*F*reedom comes only from embracing the truth about your neediness and God's provision. And what is that truth? Real truth is found in the person of Jesus Christ. He shows the reality of God, sin, salvation, eternal life, faith, and obedience. Truth is wisdom for living. What is freedom? Freedom is not the ability to do anything you want—that usually just brings you back into slavery. Freedom is the ability to live a life consistent with truth, in a way that keeps you free in heart, mind, body, and soul. True freedom is the reality of God's holiness overpowering your natural sinful inclinations and filling your life with the goodness and fullness of God's liberating love.

DIVINE PROMISE

AGAINST ITS WILL, ALL CREATION WAS SUBJECTED TO GOD'S CURSE. BUT WITH EAGER HOPE, THE CREATION LOOKS FORWARD TO THE DAY WHEN IT WILL JOIN GOD'S CHILDREN IN GLORIOUS FREEDOM FROM DEATH AND DECAY. *Romans 8:20-21*

Friendship

MY QUESTION *for* GOD

Why is it important to keep God at the center of my friendships?

A MOMENT *with* GOD

A friend is always loyal, and a brother is born to help
in time of need.   PROVERBS 17:17

Love is patient and kind. Love is not jealous or
boastful or proud or rude. It does not demand its
own way.   1 CORINTHIANS 13:4-5

Don't team up with those who are unbelievers. How
can righteousness be a partner with wickedness? How
can light live with darkness?   2 CORINTHIANS 6:14

Be kind to each other, tenderhearted, forgiving one
another, just as God through Christ has forgiven you.
                                              EPHESIANS 4:32

Paul's timeless description of Christian love applies
to all your friendships. A good friend is loyal, helpful, kind, patient, and forgiving. True friendships are
glued together with bonds of loyalty and commitment.
They remain intact despite changing external circumstances. You will probably discover that your closest
friends also share your commitment to Christ. If you
demonstrate to your friends all the characteristics God
demonstrates to you, you will always have strong and
loyal friends.

DIVINE PROMISE

[JESUS SAID,] "WHERE TWO OR THREE GATHER
TOGETHER AS MY FOLLOWERS, I AM THERE
AMONG THEM." *Matthew 18:20*

Friendship with God

MY QUESTION *for* GOD

How can I be friends with God?

A MOMENT *with* GOD

Inside the Tent of Meeting, the LORD would speak to
Moses face to face, as one speaks to a friend. . . . The
LORD replied to Moses, "I will indeed do what you
have asked, for I look favorably on you, and I know
you by name." EXODUS 33:11, 17

The LORD is a friend to those who fear him. He
teaches them his covenant. PSALM 25:14

It happened just as the Scriptures say: "Abraham
believed God, and God counted him as righteous
because of his faith." He was even called the friend
of God. JAMES 2:23

What qualities do you look for in a friend? Perhaps you
would list honesty, loyalty, or availability. God desires
these same qualities from you. He wants you to come
to him honestly about your struggles and successes, to
remain faithful and loyal to him and his Word, and to

make yourself available to spend quality time with him. If you fear separation in your own friendships—how much more should you fear separation from God? Respect him, confide in him, and remain loyal to him; he will call you his friend.

DIVINE PROMISE

I NO LONGER CALL YOU SLAVES, BECAUSE A MASTER DOESN'T CONFIDE IN HIS SLAVES. NOW YOU ARE MY FRIENDS, SINCE I HAVE TOLD YOU EVERYTHING THE FATHER TOLD ME. *John 15:15*

Fun

MY QUESTION *for* GOD

How does having fun help me experience God's blessings?

A MOMENT *with* GOD

[Nehemiah said,] "Go and celebrate with a feast . . . and share gifts of food with people who have nothing prepared. This is a sacred day before our Lord. Don't be dejected and sad, for the joy of the LORD is your strength!"   NEHEMIAH 8:10

For everything there is a season, a time for every activity under heaven. . . . A time to cry and a time to laugh. A time to grieve and a time to dance.

ECCLESIASTES 3:1, 4

The master was full of praise. "Well done, my good
and faithful servant. You have been faithful in handling
this small amount. . . . Let's celebrate together!"

MATTHEW 25:21

*J*udging from the number of feasts and festivals God
instituted for the Israelites, he intended for his people
to have fun. He desires for you to laugh and enjoy life.
This gives you a small taste of the joy you will experience in heaven. But having fun should be in balance
with work and never conflict with the moral codes
God has given you in his Word. Joy, fun, and celebration as God intended are important parts of walking
with him because they lift your spirits and help you see
the beauty and richness in life. When you find yourself
enjoying the moment, thank God for blessing you with
a taste of eternity.

DIVINE PROMISE
HE FILLS MY LIFE WITH GOOD THINGS.
Psalm 103:5

Future

MY QUESTION *for* GOD
How can I be sure God will direct my future?

A MOMENT *with* GOD

The LORD says, "I will guide you along the best
pathway for your life. I will advise you and watch
over you."   PSALM 32:8

*G*od directs your steps. Although the path may lead
you through some dark valleys or seem to take some
unnecessary detours, you will one day look back and
discover that God's way was perfect.

"I know the plans I have for you," says the LORD.
"They are plans for good and not for disaster, to give
you a future and a hope."   JEREMIAH 29:11

*W*hen you feel insecure about the future, it is easy
to doubt God's care for you. You might be tempted to
think that he is neglecting you or giving you only the
bare minimum. But your loving Creator will always
give you his best. How could a God who *is* love hold
back? Cling to this hope.

I am certain that God, who began the good work
within you, will continue his work until it is finally
finished on the day when Christ Jesus returns.

PHILIPPIANS 1:6

*G*od finishes what he starts. Don't allow your limitations or your present difficulties to blind you to the
promise that God will complete his work in you. Your
present insecurities are opportunities for God's work

in your heart. As long as he has work for you, you can
be sure he will guide you to where you need to be.

DIVINE PROMISE

YOU GUIDE ME WITH YOUR COUNSEL, LEADING
ME TO A GLORIOUS DESTINY.   *Psalm 73:24*

Generosity

MY QUESTION *for* GOD

What does generosity look like?

A MOMENT *with* GOD

[Jesus said,] "Wherever your treasure is, there the
desires of your heart will also be."   MATTHEW 6:21

While Jesus was in the Temple, he watched the rich
people dropping their gifts in the collection box.
Then a poor widow came by and dropped in two
small coins. "I tell you the truth," Jesus said, "this
poor widow has given more than all the rest of them.
For they have given a tiny part of their surplus, but
she, poor as she is, has given everything she has."

LUKE 21:1-4

You must each decide in your heart how much to give.
And don't give reluctantly or in response to pressure.
"For God loves a person who gives cheerfully."

2 CORINTHIANS 9:7

Don't forget to do good and to share with those in need. These are the sacrifices that please God.

HEBREWS 13:16

*W*ho is more generous—a billionaire who gives one million dollars to his church, or a poor single mom who gives one hundred dollars? And if you have a lot of money, does that mean you are not generous? Jesus said you can't know the answer to those questions without knowing the heart of the giver. Throughout the Bible, God doesn't focus on how much money you have but rather on how generous you are with it. One thing is clear: Where your money goes reveals what you care most about. It's not what you have but what you do with what you have that is significant, whether it's money, time, or talents. True generosity involves sacrifice, which is the key to changing your heart from stinginess to selflessness. When you realize that all you have is a gift from a generous God, it motivates you to share your material and earthly possessions more freely. Generosity is both a spiritual gift and a spiritual discipline. To some, generosity comes easy; others must work hard at it. But no one can afford to neglect it.

DIVINE PROMISE

REMEMBER THE WORDS OF THE LORD JESUS: "IT IS MORE BLESSED TO GIVE THAN TO RECEIVE."

Acts 20:35

Gentleness

MY QUESTIONS *for* GOD

What does gentleness accomplish? Won't people walk all over me if I am gentle?

A MOMENT *with* GOD

The Holy Spirit produces this kind of fruit in our lives: love, joy, peace, patience, kindness, goodness, faithfulness, gentleness, and self-control.

GALATIANS 5:22-23

Pursue righteousness and a godly life, along with faith, love, perseverance, and gentleness. 1 TIMOTHY 6:11

You should clothe yourselves instead with the beauty that comes from within, the unfading beauty of a gentle and quiet spirit, which is so precious to God.

1 PETER 3:4

*B*eing gentle does not mean that you are a doormat and let others walk all over you. God is the perfect example of gentleness, and yet he is also a mighty warrior, able to defeat the powers of hell. Gentleness may be the most powerful weapon in your arsenal. You accomplish more by gentleness than by coercion.

DIVINE PROMISE

GOD BLESSES THOSE WHO ARE HUMBLE, FOR THEY WILL INHERIT THE WHOLE EARTH.

Matthew 5:5

Giving

MY QUESTION *for* GOD

How does giving reflect the heart of God?

A MOMENT *with* GOD

Everything we have has come from you, and we give you only what you first gave us!   1 CHRONICLES 29:14

"Bring all the tithes into the storehouse so there will be enough food in my Temple. If you do," says the LORD of Heaven's Armies, "I will open the windows of heaven for you. I will pour out a blessing so great you won't have enough room to take it in! Try it! Put me to the test!"   MALACHI 3:10

God has given each of you a gift from his great variety of spiritual gifts. Use them well to serve one another.

1 PETER 4:10

Giving is a remarkable concept that originates in the heart of a generous God, who pours out more blessings on his people than we could ever deserve. The gift of life, the gift of love, the gift of salvation, the gift of eternity in heaven—all of these are priceless. The possessions you have are generally a tangible result of what you have invested through time, energy, and talent. But who you are—your character—is always a direct result of what you have invested of yourself with God and others. And one of the great and unique promises of the Bible is that the more you give, the more you receive—not necessarily in material possessions, but in spiritual and eternal rewards.

DIVINE PROMISE

GIVE, AND YOU WILL RECEIVE. YOUR GIFT
WILL RETURN TO YOU IN FULL—PRESSED
DOWN, SHAKEN TOGETHER TO MAKE ROOM
FOR MORE, RUNNING OVER, AND POURED
INTO YOUR LAP. THE AMOUNT YOU GIVE WILL
DETERMINE THE AMOUNT YOU GET BACK.
Luke 6:38

God's Call

MY QUESTION *for* GOD

How do I know what my calling is?

A MOMENT *with* GOD

Your word is a lamp to guide my feet and a light for my path.   PSALM 119:105

The first step in knowing your calling is to get to know God more closely by reading his Word. As God communicates with you through the Bible, he will show you what to do and where he wants you to go.

God gave [Daniel, Shadrach, Meshach, and Abednego] an unusual aptitude for understanding every aspect of literature and wisdom.   DANIEL 1:17

God has given each person certain aptitudes and abilities. These provide the biggest clue to what God wants you to do. When he calls you to do something for him, he will almost always allow you to use your God-given gifts to get the job done. In the meantime, develop those special abilities, and begin to use them, and you will begin to see what God wants you to do.

When God gives you a specific calling, it fills your thoughts and energies so that you have a longing to pursue it wholeheartedly.

Let God transform you into a new person by changing the way you think. Then you will learn to know God's will for you.   ROMANS 12:2

When God transforms you by the power of his Holy Spirit, he will literally begin to change the way you think so that your mind will recognize what he wants you to do.

DIVINE PROMISE
MY LIFE IS WORTH NOTHING TO ME UNLESS
I USE IT FOR FINISHING THE WORK ASSIGNED
ME BY THE LORD JESUS. *Acts 20:24*

God's Hand

In what ways can I see the hand of God working in my life?

Job replied, " . . . Should we accept only good things from the hand of God and never anything bad?" JOB 2:10

Come and see what our God has done, what awesome miracles he performs for people! PSALM 66:5

It is the LORD who provides the sun to light the day and the moon and stars to light the night, and who stirs the sea into roaring waves. His name is the LORD of Heaven's Armies. JEREMIAH 31:35

Sometimes God demonstrates his power through visible, miraculous signs. At other times his power is much more subtle, perhaps working in your heart as you seek him. Sometimes God works through events in your life or uses surprising people to accomplish his will. Sometimes God is a still, quiet voice in your mind, and at other times he is a force to be reckoned with. The point is that some things about God are constant and unchanging: his love, his law, his promises. Other things about God are wild and mysterious. He rarely works the same way twice in your life, which calls for you to be diligent in trusting him and always expectant about how he wants to work his will through you. Often, it isn't until you look back on your life that you can see God's fingerprints all over the masterpiece of your life. Trust him and watch for the ways he works, and let these be divine moments to be thankful that God's hand is on you even now.

DIVINE PROMISE

WHATEVER IS GOOD AND PERFECT COMES DOWN TO US FROM GOD OUR FATHER, WHO CREATED ALL THE LIGHTS IN THE HEAVENS.
James 1:17

God's Timing

MY QUESTION *for* GOD

What are the benefits of waiting on God's timing?

A MOMENT *with* GOD

I waited patiently for the LORD to help me, and he turned to me and heard my cry.   PSALM 40:1

I wait quietly before God, for my victory comes from him. . . . Let all that I am wait quietly before God, for my hope is in him.   PSALM 62:1, 5

This is the plan: At the right time he will bring everything together under the authority of Christ— everything in heaven and on earth.   EPHESIANS 1:10

*H*ow we hate to wait! Even trivial delays such as red lights or slow cashier lines can make us edgy, even angry. And it can be especially frustrating when God does not seem to be acting, even though we have prayed and it seems obvious that what we are praying for is right and good. It's hard to accept that God's timing is usually different from ours. And it's even harder to accept that his timing is best for us, because we can't see what's up ahead. We want what's best for us now. But the ability to wait quietly for something is evidence of a strong character. Waiting on God reflects the patient confidence that what he promises for your life now and in the future will come true. When you are able to wait quietly for God to act without becoming restless and agitated, you show that you fully trust his timing. As the old saying puts it, God is rarely early, but he's never late.

DIVINE PROMISE

REJOICE IN OUR CONFIDENT HOPE. BE PATIENT IN TROUBLE, AND KEEP ON PRAYING.   *Romans 12:12*

Goodness

MY QUESTION *for* GOD

How can I be truly good?

A MOMENT *with* GOD

Who can find a virtuous and capable wife? She is more precious than rubies. Her husband can trust her, and she will greatly enrich his life. She brings him good, not harm, all the days of her life.

PROVERBS 31:10-12

The Kingdom of God is not a matter of what we eat or drink, but of living a life of goodness and peace and joy in the Holy Spirit.   ROMANS 14:17

Goodness is not merely being talented at something, as in "she is a master gardener." Goodness is a composite of many qualities such as being kind, helpful, loving, pleasant, generous, and gentle. These qualities exhibit your likeness to God and reflect his loving nature. When God takes control of your heart, you will begin doing good deeds that, over a lifetime, will be defined as goodness.

DIVINE PROMISE

YOU ARE A CHOSEN PEOPLE. YOU ARE ROYAL PRIESTS, A HOLY NATION, GOD'S VERY OWN POSSESSION. AS A RESULT, YOU CAN SHOW OTHERS THE GOODNESS OF GOD, FOR HE CALLED YOU OUT OF THE DARKNESS INTO HIS WONDERFUL LIGHT.   *1 Peter 2:9*

Gossip

MY QUESTION *for* GOD

How can I begin to reverse the damage done by gossip?

A Moment *with* God

Gossip separates the best of friends.   PROVERBS 16:28

Rumors are dainty morsels that sink deep into
one's heart.   PROVERBS 18:8

A gossip goes around telling secrets, so don't hang
around with chatterers.   PROVERBS 20:19

Fire goes out without wood, and quarrels disappear
when gossip stops.   PROVERBS 26:20

It's fun to gossip because it makes us feel as if we're
letting others in on our little secrets. The Bible charac-
terizes bits of gossip as "dainty morsels." The problem
is, gossip is based on rumors, not facts, and gossip is
often meant to damage another's reputation, not build
it up. Everyone loves to be in on the latest news, but
the people with whom you gossip are probably also gos-
siping about you. Gossip separates friends, reveals people's secrets, and causes much hurt. Gossip puts you in
the position of judging others. In a court of law, rumors
and opinions are not allowed because they might un-
justly sway the opinion of the jury. So it is when you
turn your bedroom or kitchen into a courtroom where
you sit as judge and allow rumor and opinion to color
and often damage the reputation of others who have no
chance to defend themselves. You can make gossip stop
by changing the subject or by saying something kind
about the person being gossiped about. When you don't
add fuel, the fire will go out. Your kind words may

allow God's grace to break through to those around you and may even reach the ears of those you defend.

DIVINE PROMISE

THE SCRIPTURES SAY, "IF YOU WANT TO ENJOY LIFE AND SEE MANY HAPPY DAYS, KEEP YOUR TONGUE FROM SPEAKING EVIL AND YOUR LIPS FROM TELLING LIES." *1 Peter 3:10*

Grace

MY QUESTION *for* GOD

What is the grace of God?

A MOMENT *with* GOD

The wages of sin is death, but the free gift of God is eternal life through Christ Jesus our Lord.   ROMANS 6:23

God saved you by his grace when you believed. And you can't take credit for this; it is a gift from God. Salvation is not a reward for the good things we have done, so none of us can boast about it.   EPHESIANS 2:8-9

Grace is both a onetime act—the undeserved favor of God in giving you salvation through faith in Jesus—and a way of life—the ongoing work of God in you. Simply put, grace is God's special favor. Because of his grace, God gives you blessings you don't deserve, and in his mercy, he withholds the punishment your sins do deserve. When you understand God's grace, you will be moved to share that same acceptance and freedom with those around you and extend God's grace to them.

DIVINE PROMISE

GOD, WITH UNDESERVED KINDNESS, DECLARES THAT WE ARE RIGHTEOUS. HE DID THIS THROUGH CHRIST JESUS WHEN HE FREED US FROM THE PENALTY FOR OUR SINS.   *Romans 3:24*

Grief

MY QUESTION *for* GOD

Is there something the matter with me if I'm still feeling sad long after a great loss?

A MOMENT *with* GOD

I will never forget this awful time, as I grieve over my loss. Yet I still dare to hope when I remember this: The faithful love of the LORD never ends! His mercies never cease. Great is his faithfulness; his mercies begin afresh each morning.   LAMENTATIONS 3:20-23

Our hearts are sick and weary, and our eyes grow dim with tears.   LAMENTATIONS 5:17

*A*re you surprised that almost at the end of Lamentations, Jeremiah is still crying? Even after a stirring declaration of hope in 3:22-27 and a period of thoughtful reflection, Jeremiah's eyes fill again with tears, just as they did in previous chapters and throughout the book of Lamentations. The grief process is not swift, nor is it a steady progression. Even after a good week, a good laugh, a theological insight, or a renewal of hope, you may weep again. There is nothing wrong with you; this is part of the process of grieving and healing. Allow yourself the time to grieve, but remember that God is with you and cares about your pain.

DIVINE PROMISE

YOU KEEP TRACK OF ALL MY SORROWS. YOU HAVE COLLECTED ALL MY TEARS IN YOUR BOTTLE. YOU HAVE RECORDED EACH ONE IN YOUR BOOK.   *Psalm 56:8*

Guilt

MY QUESTION *for* GOD

How will my life change if I accept God's gift of salvation and am set free from guilt?

A MOMENT *with* GOD

When a certain immoral woman from that city heard [Jesus] was eating there, she brought a beautiful alabaster jar filled with expensive perfume. Then she knelt behind him at his feet, weeping. Her tears fell on his feet, and she wiped them off with her hair. Then she kept kissing his feet and putting perfume on them. . . . "I tell you, her sins—and they are many— have been forgiven, so she has shown me much love. But a person who is forgiven little shows only little love.". . . And Jesus said to the woman, "Your faith has saved you; go in peace."   LUKE 7:37-38, 47, 50

If we confess our sins to [God], he is faithful and just to forgive us our sins and to cleanse us from all wickedness. If we claim we have not sinned, we are calling God a liar and showing that his word has no place in our hearts.   I JOHN 1:9-10

You might know the experience of confessing your sin to God but still feeling guilty. If so, the problem is not with God but with you. God does not want you to atone for your sin by feeling guilty and miserable. Rather, you are to trust that he forgives you. Like a judge pardoning a guilty prisoner, God pardons you, and you accept his forgiveness by faith.

The immoral woman demonstrated the life-changing power of the pardon that comes from God's grace and mercy. She knew that God not only welcomed her but also forgave her. Her actions expressed her faith and her gratitude. Faith is not simply a matter of believing in the mind; it is a matter of trusting and responding to God's grace in every aspect of your life. God's love breaks the power of sin so that you are free to worship him gratefully, make costly sacrifices willingly, serve humbly, and express your faith boldly.

DIVINE PROMISE

EVEN IF WE FEEL GUILTY, GOD IS GREATER
THAN OUR FEELINGS, AND HE KNOWS
EVERYONE. *1 John 3:20*

Habits

MY QUESTION *for* GOD

Why should I make a habit of reading the Bible?

A MOMENT *with* GOD

When he sits on the throne as king, he must copy
for himself this body of instruction on a scroll. . . .
He must always keep that copy with him and read
it daily as long as he lives. That way he will learn to
fear the LORD his God by obeying all the terms of
these instructions and decrees. This regular reading
will prevent him from becoming proud and acting as
if he is above his fellow citizens. It will also prevent
him from turning away from these commands in
the smallest way. And it will ensure that he and his
descendants will reign for many generations in Israel.

DEUTERONOMY 17:18-20

Jesus told [the devil], "No! The Scriptures say,
'People do not live by bread alone, but by every word
that comes from the mouth of God.'" MATTHEW 4:4

*I*magine asking, "Should I eat regularly or just once every few days?" No, you eat to stay healthy and alive. Jesus taught that God's Word is spiritual food that you depend on for spiritual life. The Bible provides daily nourishment for your soul. This means you can't read the Bible only when you get around to it. It is only through regular Bible study that you can maintain the right perspective about sin and holiness and God's love. Without a regular habit of Bible reading, you will inevitably drift from God. And being apart from God gives you no chance to experience the mercy and blessings that come from a relationship with him.

DIVINE PROMISE

EVEN MORE BLESSED ARE ALL WHO HEAR THE
WORD OF GOD AND PUT IT INTO PRACTICE.
Luke 11:28

*H*appiness

MY QUESTION *for* GOD

Where can I find real, lasting happiness?

A MOMENT *with* GOD

Oh, the joys of those who do not follow the advice of the wicked.   PSALM 1:1

Give me happiness, O Lord, for I give myself to you.

PSALM 86:4

Joyful are people of integrity, who follow the
instructions of the LORD. Joyful are those who obey
his laws and search for him with all their hearts. They
do not compromise with evil, and they walk only in
his paths.   PSALM 119:1-3

*H*appiness comes from obeying God's Word, which
he gave to us with our best interests in mind. Many
people bring unhappiness on themselves by choosing
lifestyles that are destructive. Someone craving acceptance and love may choose sexual involvement outside
marriage, which leads to pain and emotional scars, the
natural consequence of intimacy without commitment.
Someone else may believe that exorbitant wealth is so
important that it's worth using dishonest means to ac-
quire it. But true, long-term happiness is cultivated by
following the principles God designed for your long-
term well-being. God graciously provides positive,
healthful life principles through his Word. It is by doing what is right that you can enjoy life without fear of
how it will turn out.

DIVINE PROMISE

DO WHAT IS RIGHT AND GOOD IN THE
LORD'S SIGHT, SO ALL WILL GO WELL
WITH YOU.   *Deuteronomy 6:18*

Hard-Heartedness

MY QUESTION *for* GOD

What are the signs of a hard heart?

A MOMENT *with* GOD

Pharaoh's heart, however, remained hard. He still
refused to listen, just as the LORD had predicted.

EXODUS 7:13

"Oh no, sir!" [Hannah] replied. "I haven't been
drinking wine or anything stronger. But I am very
discouraged, and I was pouring out my heart to
the LORD."   1 SAMUEL 1:15

The older brother was angry and wouldn't go in.
His father came out and begged him, but he replied,
"All these years I've slaved for you and never once
refused to do a single thing you told me to. And
in all that time you never gave me even one young
goat for a feast with my friends. Yet when this son
of yours comes back after squandering your money
on prostitutes, you celebrate by killing the fattened
calf!" His father said to him, "Look, dear son, you
have always stayed by me, and everything I have is
yours. We had to celebrate this happy day. For your
brother was dead and has come back to life! He was
lost, but now he is found!"   LUKE 15:28-32

Pharaoh had a hard, stubborn heart. No matter how
much he heard about God or how many miracles he
saw, he refused to believe. The older brother of the

Prodigal Son also struggled with a hard heart; he was
more eager to punish than to forgive. Hannah, however,
continued to pray to God even when nothing seemed
to happen. As you evaluate the condition of your heart,
you must always ask whether it is becoming more hard
and stubborn or more soft and pliable, reaching out to
God whatever your circumstances. If you find it hard
to forgive others when they ask for it, or if you struggle
to see God in your daily life, then your heart may be
hardening. If you let it continue, you cut yourself off
from God, your lifeline to the only One who can really
help you. A hard heart rejects the only thing that can
save it—God's love. A soft heart will seek God's help
and notice his perfectly timed responses.

DIVINE PROMISE

I WILL GIVE YOU A NEW HEART, AND I WILL
PUT A NEW SPIRIT IN YOU. I WILL TAKE OUT
YOUR STONY, STUBBORN HEART AND GIVE YOU
A TENDER, RESPONSIVE HEART. *Ezekiel 36:26*

Healing

MY QUESTION *for* GOD

Will God heal the hurts in my life?

A Moment *with* God

For you who fear my name, the Sun of Righteousness will rise with healing in his wings. And you will go free, leaping with joy like calves let out to pasture.

MALACHI 4:2

Moved with compassion, Jesus reached out and touched him. "I am willing," he said. "Be healed!"

MARK 1:41

*H*e who made your body can certainly repair and restore it. He who made your mind can repair and restore it, too. He who made your soul can also repair and restore it. God is not bound by the limitations of this world. He can intervene to overcome any threat to your life, including illness and disease—physical, mental, spiritual, and emotional. You know from God's Word that he loves you enough to die for you. He promises that in eternity you will be fully healed. With assurance of his love for you and the hope of his promise of ultimate healing, you have what you need to endure and wait for God's healing power to make you whole—whether in this life or in eternity.

Divine Promise

I HEARD A LOUD SHOUT FROM THE THRONE, SAYING, "LOOK, GOD'S HOME IS NOW AMONG HIS PEOPLE! HE WILL LIVE WITH THEM, AND THEY WILL BE HIS PEOPLE. GOD HIMSELF WILL BE WITH THEM. HE WILL WIPE EVERY

TEAR FROM THEIR EYES, AND THERE WILL BE
NO MORE DEATH OR SORROW OR CRYING
OR PAIN." *Revelation 21:3-4*

Health

MY QUESTIONS *for* GOD

*Does God care about my physical health? Isn't spiritual
health more important to him?*

A MOMENT *with* GOD

Don't you realize that your body is the temple of the
Holy Spirit, who lives in you and was given to you by
God? You do not belong to yourself, for God bought
you with a high price. So you must honor God with
your body.   1 CORINTHIANS 6:19-20

Physical training is good, but training for godliness is
much better, promising benefits in this life and in the
life to come.   1 TIMOTHY 4:8

God is concerned about both. Your Creator knows
that your spiritual disciplines—worship, prayer, obedience to God's Word—have a profound impact on your
physical life, and that your physical habits—from nu-
trition to hygiene—influence your spiritual life. God's
presence in your life should affect what you do and say.
You must remember that God cares deeply about the
condition of both your body and your soul. Spiritual
exercise is as purposeful and strenuous as physical exer-

cise. But it is important to remember that the benefits of spiritual fitness last for eternity while the benefits of physical fitness last only as long as your body. Knowing the eternally long-term benefits of spiritual exercise should motivate you to keep your physical and spiritual health in a wholesome balance and help you to experience a vibrant relationship with your Creator.

DIVINE PROMISE

THE LORD WILL GUIDE YOU CONTINUALLY, GIVING YOU WATER WHEN YOU ARE DRY AND RESTORING YOUR STRENGTH. YOU WILL BE LIKE A WELL-WATERED GARDEN, LIKE AN EVER-FLOWING SPRING. *Isaiah 58:11*

Heart

MY QUESTION *for* GOD

How can my heart become the kind of heart God can use?

A MOMENT *with* GOD

When the LORD saw their change of heart, he gave this message to Shemaiah: "Since the people have humbled themselves, I will not completely destroy them and will soon give them some relief."

2 CHRONICLES 12:7

Develop an attitude of humility. Only when you are humble can you begin to change into a person God can use.

Put all your rebellion behind you, and find yourselves a new heart and a new spirit.   EZEKIEL 18:31

Get rid of any sinful habit or lifestyle. Practice obeying God's Word, and you will see your heart change for the better.

Let the Spirit renew your thoughts and attitudes. Put on your new nature, created to be like God—truly righteous and holy.   EPHESIANS 4:23-24

You harvest what you plant. Pumpkin seeds produce pumpkins. Sunflower seeds produce sunflowers. That is exactly why you must ask the Lord to plant a pure and obedient spirit within your heart, so that your life will produce clean thoughts, actions, and motives.

Wherever your treasure is, there the desires of your heart will also be.   LUKE 12:34

When God is the center of your life, your relationship with him will be your highest priority. You will long to spend time in prayer and reading the Bible. Your thoughts will often turn to God; you will want to please him, and you will want to obey him. The more you love God, the more your heart will long to be closer to his.

DIVINE PROMISE

CREATE IN ME A CLEAN HEART, O GOD. RENEW A LOYAL SPIRIT WITHIN ME. *Psalm 51:10*

Help

MY QUESTION *for* GOD

I can't do everything all by myself. Where can I find the help I need?

A MOMENT *with* GOD

The LORD God said, "It is not good for the man to be alone. I will make a helper who is just right for him."

GENESIS 2:18

Whenever they were in trouble and turned to the LORD, the God of Israel, and sought him out, they found him.   2 CHRONICLES 15:4

The LORD is my strength and shield. I trust him with all my heart. He helps me, and my heart is filled with joy.   PSALM 28:7

This same God who takes care of me will supply all your needs from his glorious riches, which have been given to us in Christ Jesus.   PHILIPPIANS 4:19

*E*veryone has limitations—areas of weakness, feelings of inadequacy, a lack of skill or knowledge. Sometimes you just don't know what to do or how to do it. Sometimes a crisis strikes, and you just can't handle it by yourself. You need help. Although our culture may admire the strong independent spirit, no one can really survive alone. That's why God created you to be in relationship with him and with other people. Part of relationship is giving and receiving help. You need help to get work done. You need help to restore a relationship. You need help to develop your skills. You need help to think through a problem. You need help to say, "I'm sorry." God wants to help you too. He is the ultimate helper, for he is wiser, stronger, and infinitely loving. Not only does your help come from God, but God also promises to help those who help others. Cultivate the habit of seeking the help of both God and others and of offering help to those in need.

DIVINE PROMISE

COMMIT EVERYTHING YOU DO TO THE LORD.
TRUST HIM, AND HE WILL HELP YOU.   *Psalm 37:5*

Helplessness

MY QUESTION *for* GOD

How can I find hope when there's nothing I can do?

A MOMENT *with* GOD

Asa cried out to the LORD his God, "O LORD, no one
but you can help the powerless against the mighty!
Help us, O LORD our God, for we trust in you alone.
It is in your name that we have come against this vast
horde. O LORD, you are our God; do not let mere
men prevail against you!"   2 CHRONICLES 14:11

You see the trouble and grief they cause. You take
note of it and punish them. The helpless put their
trust in you. You defend the orphans. . . . LORD, you
know the hopes of the helpless. Surely you will hear
their cries and comfort them.   PSALM 10:14, 17

The LORD is my strength and shield. I trust him with
all my heart. He helps me, and my heart is filled with
joy. I burst out in songs of thanksgiving.   PSALM 28:7

*W*hen you ask God for help, and trust that he will
help, you open the lifeline to the One who loves doing
the impossible! If you insist on trying to get yourself
out of trouble, you will never see what God can do.

I take pleasure in my weaknesses, and in the insults,
hardships, persecutions, and troubles that I suffer for
Christ. For when I am weak, then I am strong.

2 CORINTHIANS 12:10

*L*ook at the situation from God's perspective. As long
as you look through eyes of helplessness, you will see
only your hopeless condition and you blind yourself to

the many ways in which God may already be helping you. When you look through the eyes of faith in God, you will find hope and help.

Because you are my helper, I sing for joy in the shadow of your wings.

PSALM 63:7

Rejoice as you remember how God has helped you in the past, and be assured of his presence and protection in the future. He who walked with the saints of the past is here with you today and tomorrow.

DIVINE PROMISE

I LOOK UP TO THE MOUNTAINS—DOES MY HELP COME FROM THERE? MY HELP COMES FROM THE LORD, WHO MADE HEAVEN AND EARTH! ... THE LORD KEEPS WATCH OVER YOU AS YOU COME AND GO, BOTH NOW AND FOREVER.

Psalm 121:1-2, 8

Holiness

MY QUESTION *for* GOD

What does it mean to be holy and to live a holy life?

A MOMENT *with* GOD

I plead with you to give your bodies to God because of all he has done for you. Let them be a living and holy sacrifice—the kind he will find acceptable.

ROMANS 12:1

I am writing . . . to you who have been called by
God to be his own holy people. He made you holy
by means of Christ Jesus, just as he did for all people
everywhere who call on the name of our Lord
Jesus Christ.   1 CORINTHIANS 1:2

You were cleansed; you were made holy.

1 CORINTHIANS 6:11

Think of holiness as both a journey and a final destination. To be completely holy is to be sinless, pure, and
perfect before God. Of course, no one is perfect, so
that is your ultimate goal, your final destination when
you stand before God in heaven. But holiness also
means being different, "set apart" by God for a specific
purpose. You are to be different from the rest of the
world, and your life is a journey toward becoming a
little more pure and sinless with each passing day. If
you strive to be holy during your earthly journey, you
will one day arrive at your final destination and stand
before God in holiness.

DIVINE PROMISE

EVEN BEFORE HE MADE THE WORLD, GOD
LOVED US AND CHOSE US IN CHRIST TO BE
HOLY AND WITHOUT FAULT IN HIS EYES.

Ephesians 1:4

Holy Spirit

MY QUESTION for GOD

How does the Holy Spirit—the presence of God—help me?

A MOMENT with GOD

We have received God's Spirit (not the world's spirit), so we can know the wonderful things God has freely given us.   1 CORINTHIANS 2:12

*T*he Holy Spirit is God's presence in you, helping you to understand the deep truths of God and to discover and know the mysteries and wonders of his character.

Let the Holy Spirit guide your lives. Then you won't be doing what your sinful nature craves. The sinful nature wants to do evil, which is just the opposite of what the Spirit wants. And the Spirit gives us desires that are the opposite of what the sinful nature desires.

GALATIANS 5:16-17

*T*he Holy Spirit helps you know the truth about sin and convicts you of it. It is God in you showing you right from wrong, good from bad, and his way versus the way of the world. It's amazing that God cares enough to give you one-on-one instruction on how to live a life that pleases him.

The Holy Spirit helps us in our weakness. For example, we don't know what God wants us to pray for. But the Holy Spirit prays for us with groanings that cannot be expressed in words. And the Father who knows all hearts knows what the Spirit is saying, for the Spirit pleads for us believers in harmony with God's own will. ROMANS 8:26-27

*T*he Holy Spirit helps you pray. You can take great comfort and confidence in the fact that God hears, understands, and responds to your prayers. When your soul longs to be recognized and understood and yet you can't find the right words, the Holy Spirit understands your deepest longings and expresses them to God on your behalf.

DIVINE PROMISE

THE SPIRIT IS GOD'S GUARANTEE THAT HE WILL GIVE US THE INHERITANCE HE PROMISED AND THAT HE HAS PURCHASED US TO BE HIS OWN PEOPLE. HE DID THIS SO WE WOULD PRAISE AND GLORIFY HIM. *Ephesians 1:14*

Home

MY QUESTION *for* GOD

How can I make my home a warm and inviting place?

A MOMENT *with* GOD

As soon as Laban heard that his nephew Jacob had arrived, he ran out to meet him. He embraced and kissed him and brought him home. When Jacob had told him his story, Laban exclaimed, "You really are my own flesh and blood!"   GENESIS 29:13-14

Do to others whatever you would like them to do to you.   MATTHEW 7:12

Cheerfully share your home with those who need a meal or a place to stay. God has given each of you a gift from his great variety of spiritual gifts. Use them well to serve one another.   1 PETER 4:9-10

The welcome mat by your front door is more than a symbol of entry; it is a transition from outside to inside, from stranger to friend. When people enter your home, do all you can to make them feel welcome and wanted. Greet them warmly, and focus on their needs. Are they hungry or thirsty? Do they need a listening ear or a sympathetic heart? Maybe they've come for encouragement or friendship. Your decorating, menu, and level of tidiness are not as important as the love you lavish on your guests. Good hospitality is a foretaste of the ultimate hospitality of God's warm welcome of you into his heavenly home. Your hospitality may be the way in which another person understands and accepts God's warm invitation to join him in his eternal home—heaven.

DIVINE PROMISE

THE LORD ... BLESSES THE HOME OF THE UPRIGHT. *Proverbs 3:33*

Hope

MY QUESTION *for* GOD

How does having hope in God carry me through difficult times?

A MOMENT *with* GOD

Let us hold tightly without wavering to the hope we affirm, for God can be trusted to keep his promise.

HEBREWS 10:23

When everything else is falling apart, cling to the fact that God keeps his Word. And one of the things he promises is that in heaven all your problems and suffering will be over and never again will you grieve or be discouraged.

[Jesus said,] "Don't let your hearts be troubled. Trust in God, and trust also in me." JOHN 14:1

[Jesus said,] "I have told you all this so that you may have peace in me. Here on earth you will have many trials and sorrows. But take heart, because I have overcome the world." JOHN 16:33

Your troubles do not surprise God and should not surprise you. Trouble is a fact of life in this fallen world. Instead of focusing on the problems, look to the One who experienced all the same troubles you experience and shows you how to have peace in spite of them.

Hope in the LORD; for with the LORD there is unfailing love. His redemption overflows.   PSALM 130:7

The Bible assures you that God will either deliver you from your troubles or bring you through them—for his glory and your joy.

We can rejoice, too, when we run into problems and trials, for we know that they help us develop endurance. And endurance develops strength of character, and character strengthens our confident hope of salvation. And this hope will not lead to disappointment. For we know how dearly God loves us, because he has given us the Holy Spirit to fill our hearts with his love.   ROMANS 5:3-5

Troubled times teach endurance—and strengthen your character. You will become a stronger person and more godly as you learn to endure your problems with God's help.

DIVINE PROMISE

"I KNOW THE PLANS I HAVE FOR YOU," SAYS THE
LORD. "THEY ARE PLANS FOR GOOD AND NOT
FOR DISASTER, TO GIVE YOU A FUTURE AND
A HOPE." *Jeremiah 29:11*

Hospitality

MY QUESTION *for* GOD

What do I possibly have to share with others?

A MOMENT *with* GOD

As Jesus and the disciples continued on their
way to Jerusalem, they came to a certain village
where a woman named Martha welcomed them
into her home. Her sister, Mary, sat at the Lord's
feet, listening to what he taught. But Martha was
distracted by the big dinner she was preparing. She
came to Jesus and said, "Lord, doesn't it seem unfair
to you that my sister just sits here while I do all the
work? Tell her to come and help me." But the Lord
said to her, "My dear Martha, you are worried and
upset over all these details! There is only one thing
worth being concerned about. Mary has discovered
it, and it will not be taken away from her."

LUKE 10:38-42

The most important part of hospitality is sharing
yourself and the love of God with others. The Bible

mentions both elaborate meals (see Genesis 18:1-8; 2 Samuel 3:20) and spontaneous get-togethers (see Acts 10:23). Don't be intimidated by the idea of hospitality and think that you must prepare big meals and clean the house. Just share what you have generously, and enjoy the people you are with. It is your presence, not your presentation, that makes others feel welcome.

DIVINE PROMISE

DON'T FORGET TO SHOW HOSPITALITY TO STRANGERS, FOR SOME WHO HAVE DONE THIS HAVE ENTERTAINED ANGELS WITHOUT REALIZING IT! *Hebrews 13:2*

Hurts

MY QUESTION *for* GOD

How can I find healing from the hurts in my relationships—both hurts from others and hurts I've caused?

A MOMENT *with* GOD

Don't say, "I will get even for this wrong." Wait for the LORD to handle the matter.   PROVERBS 20:22

If you forgive those who sin against you, your heavenly Father will forgive you. But if you refuse to forgive others, your Father will not forgive your sins.

MATTHEW 6:14-15

Make allowance for each other's faults, and forgive anyone who offends you. Remember, the Lord forgave you, so you must forgive others. COLOSSIANS 3:13

All of you should be of one mind. Sympathize with each other. Love each other as brothers and sisters. Be tenderhearted, and keep a humble attitude. Don't repay evil for evil. Don't retaliate with insults when people insult you. Instead, pay them back with a blessing. That is what God has called you to do, and he will bless you for it.   1 PETER 3:8-9

As you wrestle with your hurts, it is helpful to keep two things in mind: First, God's model of unconditional love shows you the importance of avoiding intentionally hurting others. This happens most often with your words, either when you use them to get what you want or when you retaliate when others hurt you first. Second, you must practice the art of forgiveness. Whether you need to apologize for hurting someone or to forgive someone who has hurt you, true forgiveness is the best antidote for melting away the hard feelings and experiencing the joy of restoration. Remember that God, the one you've hurt the most, has already offered you his complete forgiveness and desires to fully restore your relationship with him. When you are hurt by a friend, loved one, or even a stranger, it is a reminder that you long for a more perfect relationship with the One who will never hurt or disappoint you.

DIVINE PROMISE

HE HEALS THE BROKENHEARTED AND BANDAGES THEIR WOUNDS. *Psalm 147:3*

Inspiration

MY QUESTION *for* GOD

How can I inspire others to follow God?

A MOMENT *with* GOD

I heard the Lord asking, "Whom should I send as a messenger to this people? Who will go for us?" I said, "Here I am. Send me."   ISAIAH 6:8

When Daniel learned that the law had been signed, he went home and knelt down as usual in his upstairs room, with its windows open toward Jerusalem. He prayed three times a day, just as he had always done.

DANIEL 6:10

God has given you the freedom to make your own choices, and it is your responsibility to make the right ones. Choose to stand up for God and his way of life. Be fiercely committed to obeying his Word no matter what, and live out the purpose he has for your life, even in the face of great danger. Always do the right thing, and never compromise. Follow God fearlessly, and serve him faithfully, as the prophets of old did. Be the one to take a stand, and your example will inspire others to follow.

DIVINE PROMISE

DON'T BE AFRAID, FOR I AM WITH YOU.
DON'T BE DISCOURAGED, FOR I AM YOUR GOD.
I WILL STRENGTHEN YOU AND HELP YOU.
I WILL HOLD YOU UP WITH MY VICTORIOUS
RIGHT HAND.   *Isaiah 41:10*

Integrity

MY QUESTION *for* GOD

What does it mean to be a person of integrity?

A MOMENT *with* GOD

The LORD rewarded me for doing right. He has seen
my innocence. To the faithful you show yourself
faithful; to those with integrity you show integrity.

PSALM 18:24-25

[The Lord said,] "I will bring that group through
the fire and make them pure. I will refine them like
silver and purify them like gold. They will call on
my name, and I will answer them. I will say, 'These
are my people,' and they will say, 'The LORD is our
God.'"   ZECHARIAH 13:9

If you are faithful in little things, you will be faithful
in large ones. But if you are dishonest in little things,
you won't be honest with greater responsibilities.

LUKE 16:10

*I*ntegrity is essentially the unity between your character and the character of God. This union results in greater purity of heart, mind, and actions, and reflects the heart, mind, and actions of God. But integrity isn't something you can achieve instantly; developing it is a process. Just as fire is necessary to refine gold, the heat of pressure and troubles refines your integrity. Every day is a refining process that tests how pure you are becoming. If in your testing, God finds your heart and actions becoming increasingly like his in purity, then you are living more and more in union with God and are growing in integrity. Like the psalmist, don't boast in this accomplishment, but thank God for giving you the power, privilege, and direction to live according to God's ways.

DIVINE PROMISE

I KNOW, MY GOD, THAT YOU EXAMINE OUR HEARTS AND REJOICE WHEN YOU FIND INTEGRITY THERE.   *1 Chronicles 29:17*

Intercession

MY QUESTION *for* GOD

Does it really make a difference when others pray for me or I pray for others?

A Moment *with* God

Abraham said, "Lord, please don't be angry with
me if I speak one more time. Suppose only ten are
found there?" And the LORD replied, "Then I will not
destroy it for the sake of the ten."   GENESIS 18:32

While Peter was in prison, the church prayed very
earnestly for him.   ACTS 12:5

You are helping us by praying for us.   2 CORINTHIANS 1:11

*I*ntercessory prayer—praying for the needs of others—is one of the most effective tools believers have for
helping each other. It is easy to become discouraged if
you think there is nothing you can do to help someone
you care about. But the most important thing you can
do for others, and others can do for you, is to pray. Paul
was convinced that the Corinthians' prayers were vitally
connected to his deliverance by God. As the believers
were holding an all-night prayer meeting, God sent an
angel to rescue Peter from prison. And Abraham inter-
ceded effectively for an entire city. In ways beyond our
understanding, intercessory prayer is a channel for the
love and power of God, and it creates a deep bond of
fellowship between human beings as well.

Divine Promise

THE EARNEST PRAYER OF A RIGHTEOUS
PERSON HAS GREAT POWER AND PRODUCES
WONDERFUL RESULTS.   *James 5:16*

Intimacy

MY QUESTION for GOD

How can I cultivate intimate relationships?

A MOMENT with GOD

"When that day comes," says the LORD, "you will call me 'my husband' instead of 'my master.' . . . I will make you my wife forever, showing you righteousness and justice, unfailing love and compassion. I will be faithful to you and make you mine, and you will finally know me as the LORD."   HOSEA 2:16, 19-20

The LORD your God is living among you. . . . He will rejoice over you with joyful songs.   ZEPHANIAH 3:17

Being connected heart to heart, mind to mind, and soul to soul—this is intimacy. Relational intimacy, where two people become soul mates, allows you to openly share all your burdens, fears, and joys with each other. Physical intimacy is reserved for marriage, where a man and a woman, through their physical relationship, reach new heights of vulnerability that allow them to communicate at the most profound level. And above all, there is intimacy with God, where you learn about the very heart of God. God is the source of love, the only One who could create you with the ability to love. Therefore, no one knows as much about love as God does. Intimacy with God means experiencing his love to the fullest and returning that love to him. As you do this, intimacy in all your other relationships takes on new and greater meaning.

DIVINE PROMISE

MY HEART HAS HEARD YOU SAY, "COME AND
TALK WITH ME." AND MY HEART RESPONDS,
"LORD, I AM COMING."   *Psalm 27:8*

Invitation

MY QUESTION *for* GOD

How does Jesus invite me to experience him?

A MOMENT *with* GOD

Jesus called out to them, "Come, follow me, and I
will show you how to fish for people!" And they left
their nets at once and followed him.   MATTHEW 4:19-20

The invitation and promise of Jesus are clear, but they
remain only opportunities until you decide to accept
them. If Peter and Andrew had merely listened and
then said, "That's a very interesting invitation, maybe
we can talk about it again after fishing season," they
would not have become Jesus' disciples. Jesus' invitation requires a decision: to follow him or to remain
where you are. Acceptance of his invitation leads to
action; the disciples left their nets and followed Jesus. God is extending such invitations to you. Have
you given an RSVP that says, "Invitation accepted with
gratitude!"?

DIVINE PROMISE

GOD WILL DO THIS, FOR HE IS FAITHFUL TO
DO WHAT HE SAYS, AND HE HAS INVITED
YOU INTO PARTNERSHIP WITH HIS SON, JESUS
CHRIST OUR LORD.   *1 Corinthians 1:9*

Joy

MY QUESTION *for* GOD

How does knowing God inspire joy?

A MOMENT *with* GOD

You will show me the way of life, granting me the joy
of your presence and the pleasures of living with you
forever.   PSALM 16:11

Since we have been made right in God's sight by faith,
we have peace with God because of what Jesus Christ
our Lord has done for us. Because of our faith, Christ
has brought us into this place of undeserved privilege
where we now stand, and we confidently and joyfully
look forward to sharing God's glory.   ROMANS 5:1-2

We can rejoice in our wonderful new relationship
with God because our Lord Jesus Christ has made us
friends of God.   ROMANS 5:11

[The Macedonian believers] are being tested by many
troubles, and they are very poor. But they are also
filled with abundant joy, which has overflowed in rich
generosity.   2 CORINTHIANS 8:2

*J*oy happens in two ways. There is the temporary joy that is a reaction to happy events, and there is the strong and lasting joy that you experience in spite of circumstances. This lasting joy comes only as people follow God and live with his attitudes toward life. Happiness based on events is a good part of life, but if that is all you can count on, you have to keep creating happy events to keep you upbeat. Those who know the joy that comes from God don't need perpetual events to keep them happy. They experience inner joy in spite of circumstances, because they know that no matter what happens, God offers hope and promise. God does not promise constant happiness; in fact, the Bible assures you that problems will come your way because you live in a fallen world. But God does promise lasting joy for all who faithfully follow him.

DIVINE PROMISE
THE JOY OF THE LORD IS YOUR STRENGTH!
Nehemiah 8:10

Kindness

MY QUESTION *for* GOD
I think I'm kind, but what does kindness look like to God?

A MOMENT *with* GOD

There was a believer in Joppa named Tabitha (which
in Greek is Dorcas). She was always doing kind things
for others and helping the poor.   ACTS 9:36

*T*rue kindness is not limited to a single act. It is a lifestyle. Begin showing kindness in the small things you
do and say until you are truly kind in all situations.

"If you see your neighbor's ox or sheep or goat
wandering away, don't ignore your responsibility.
Take it back to its owner. . . . If you see that your
neighbor's donkey or ox has collapsed on the road,
do not look the other way. Go and help your neighbor
get it back on its feet!   DEUTERONOMY 22:1, 4

*K*indness does not look the other way and ignore the
needy; rather, it is attentive and sensitive in responding
to the needs of others.

The people of the island were very kind to us. It was
cold and rainy, so they built a fire on the shore to
welcome us.   ACTS 28:2-3

*K*indness looks for opportunities to help when others
are experiencing trouble and hardship.

Make allowance for each other's faults, and forgive
anyone who offends you. Remember, the Lord
forgave you, so you must forgive others. COLOSSIANS 3:13

Don't retaliate with insults when people insult you.
Instead, pay them back with a blessing. That is what
God has called you to do, and he will bless you for it.

1 PETER 3:8-9

*K*indness shows forgiveness and mercy to others,
even when they don't deserve it.

John replied, "If you have two shirts, give one to
the poor. If you have food, share it with those who
are hungry."

LUKE 3:11

Don't forget to show hospitality to strangers, for
some who have done this have entertained angels
without realizing it!

HEBREWS 13:2

*K*indness is generously sharing what you have with
others and helping those who need your help even
when you don't know them.

A servant of the Lord must not quarrel but must be
kind to everyone, be able to teach, and be patient
with difficult people.

2 TIMOTHY 2:24

*K*indness confronts and teaches others to be peace-
loving and patient.

Don't use foul or abusive language. Let everything
you say be good and helpful, so that your words will
be an encouragement to those who hear them.

EPHESIANS 4:29

*K*indness is using encouraging, helpful words rather than foul or criticizing words.

*Y*our acts of kindness do not need to be major, award-winning events. God sees and rewards every act of kindness.

DIVINE PROMISE

[JESUS SAID,] "IF YOU GIVE EVEN A CUP OF COLD WATER TO ONE OF THE LEAST OF MY FOLLOWERS, YOU WILL SURELY BE REWARDED."
Matthew 10:42

Letting Go

MY QUESTION *for* GOD

How can I do better at letting go of certain things and trusting God with them?

A MOMENT *with* GOD

Pharaoh gave this order to all his people: "Throw every newborn Hebrew boy into the Nile River. But you may let the girls live." . . . About this time, a man and woman from the tribe of Levi got married. The woman became pregnant and gave birth to a son. She saw that he was a special baby and kept him hidden for three months. But when she could no longer hide

him, she got a basket made of papyrus reeds and
waterproofed it with tar and pitch. She put the baby
in the basket and laid it among the reeds along the
bank of the Nile River. The baby's sister then stood
at a distance, watching to see what would happen to
him. Soon Pharaoh's daughter came down to bathe
in the river, and her attendants walked along the
riverbank. When the princess saw the basket among
the reeds, she sent her maid to get it for her. When
the princess opened it, she saw the baby. The little
boy was crying, and she felt sorry for him. "This must
be one of the Hebrew children," she said. Then the
baby's sister approached the princess. "Should I go
and find one of the Hebrew women to nurse the baby
for you?" she asked. "Yes, do!" the princess replied.
So the girl went and called the baby's mother. "Take
this baby and nurse him for me," the princess told the
baby's mother. "I will pay you for your help." So the
woman took her baby home and nursed him.

EXODUS 1:22; 2:1-9

*P*haraoh's decree meant that all the Hebrews' male
children were in danger and would die. Moses' parents
cared for him as long as they could, so that he had some
strength, but then they had to literally let him go and en-
trust him to God's care as they placed him in the basket.
They showed us how to let go and trust God in situations
that are beyond our control. We do what we know is
right to do for as long as we can, and then we trust God
to take it from there. The more we try to control a situation, the less we hold on to God. Letting go means that

sometimes we serve God when we obediently stand and watch. Moses' mother let go of her baby's basket on the water, but she did not let go of her care and concern for him. Because she was alert and prepared, God gave her the opportunity to do more than she ever could have hoped for. Letting go does not mean giving up. It means watching for God's next move. So if God says stand and watch him work, we stand and watch him work. If he says move, then we move with him! Both are equal in obedience and service.

DIVINE PROMISE

[THE LORD SAID,] "CALL ON ME WHEN YOU ARE IN TROUBLE, AND I WILL RESCUE YOU, AND YOU WILL GIVE ME GLORY." *Psalm 50:15*

Limitations

MY QUESTION *for* GOD

What does God think when he looks at me with all my faults and limitations?

A MOMENT *with* GOD

The angel of the LORD came and sat beneath the great tree at Ophrah, which belonged to Joash of the clan of Abiezer. Gideon son of Joash was threshing wheat at the bottom of a winepress to hide the grain from the Midianites. The angel of the LORD appeared to him and said, "Mighty hero, the LORD is with you!"

JUDGES 6:11-12

*T*he angel of the Lord greeted Gideon by calling him a mighty hero. Was God talking to the right person? This was Gideon, the man hiding from his enemies in a winepress, the man who claimed he was "the least" of his family (see Judges 6:15). Yet God called him a mighty hero. God's message to Gideon—and to you— is clear: You are more than what you have become. God calls out the best in you. He sees more in you than you see in yourself. You may look at your limitations; but God looks at your potential. If you want to increase your possibilities, learn to see life from God's perspective. He doesn't put nearly as many limitations on you as you do. He sees you for what he intended you to be, what he created you to be. How encouraging that the almighty God of the universe looks at you for what you can become in him rather than for what you are. What are you hiding from? In what areas is God calling out more from you?

DIVINE PROMISE

ALL GLORY TO GOD, WHO IS ABLE, THROUGH HIS MIGHTY POWER AT WORK WITHIN US, TO ACCOMPLISH INFINITELY MORE THAN WE MIGHT ASK OR THINK. *Ephesians 3:20*

Listening

MY QUESTION *for* GOD

How can I know that God is listening to my prayers?

A MOMENT *with* GOD

The LORD is far from the wicked, but he hears the
prayers of the righteous.   PROVERBS 15:29

Devote yourselves to prayer with an alert mind and a
thankful heart.   COLOSSIANS 4:2

Sometimes it may feel as if your prayers are bounc-
ing off the ceiling. Is God paying attention? The bigger
question is this: Are you paying attention? God does
answer prayer, and he wants to do so because he is loving and good. It's his nature to give good things to his
people. But, after a problem is resolved, you may fail
to give God the credit because you didn't notice that
he answered! When you pray, be alert and watch for
God's response, even if it isn't what you expected. And
don't forget to thank him for it, because no matter what
it is, you can be sure that it is in your best interest.

DIVINE PROMISE

THE EYES OF THE LORD WATCH OVER THOSE
WHO DO RIGHT, AND HIS EARS ARE OPEN TO
THEIR PRAYERS.   *1 Peter 3:12*

Listening

My Question *for* God

What are the blessings of being a good listener?

A Moment *with* God

"What have you done?" Joseph demanded. "Don't you know that a man like me can predict the future?"

GENESIS 44:15

*K*nowledge: Good listening involves asking questions, because the answers provide important information. Joseph wanted to listen to how his brothers answered his question, because their answer would reveal whether their hearts had changed. A good listener is always blessed with more knowledge to make godly decisions and to nurture godly relationships with others.

If you listen to correction, you grow in understanding.

PROVERBS 15:32

*M*aturity: Good listening involves being open to advice. To grow in understanding you need to be willing to accept godly correction when you make mistakes. Listening involves a willingness to hear and learn, not just about others, but also about yourself. Being a good listener brings the blessings of spiritual maturity.

The heart of the godly thinks carefully before speaking.

PROVERBS 15:28

$\mathcal{S}$elf-Control: Listening often involves talking less and then choosing your words carefully when you do speak. When you speak less, you encourage others to share more, and you provide a safe environment for them to bare their struggles to you.

DIVINE PROMISE

COME AND LISTEN TO MY COUNSEL. I'LL SHARE MY HEART WITH YOU AND MAKE YOU WISE.
Proverbs 1:23

$\mathcal{L}$oneliness

MY QUESTION *for* GOD

How can God help me when I'm feeling lonely?

A MOMENT *with* GOD

[Elisha] went in alone and shut the door behind him and prayed to the LORD.   2 KINGS 4:33

Even when I walk through the darkest valley, I will not be afraid, for you are close beside me. Your rod and your staff protect and comfort me.   PSALM 23:4

How precious are your thoughts about me, O God. They cannot be numbered!   PSALM 139:17

The LORD is close to all who call on him, yes, to all who call on him in truth.   PSALM 145:18

*E*ven when you feel alone, God is always with you. He is thinking about you all the time. Don't give up on him when you are lonely. Don't abandon all relationships because a few have failed. Doing so will cause you to feel sorry for yourself and become discouraged. Use this "alone time" to discover the faithfulness of God. As you do, you will be compelled to reach out to others, even when you have been abandoned. Getting involved with others takes the focus off your lonely feelings and places it on another's well-being. Put yourself in places where you can meet and get to know people. The church is a great place to start.

DIVINE PROMISE

THOSE WHO KNOW YOUR NAME TRUST IN YOU, FOR YOU, O LORD, DO NOT ABANDON THOSE WHO SEARCH FOR YOU. *Psalm 9:10*

Loss

MY QUESTION *for* GOD

How do I deal with loss in my life?

A MOMENT *with* GOD

"Where have you put him?" [Jesus] asked them. They told him, "Lord, come and see." Then Jesus wept. The people who were standing nearby said, "See how much he loved him!"

JOHN 11:34-36

*D*on't deny your loss. Jesus' tears over the death of Lazarus forever validate your tears of grief.

The Egyptians mourned [Jacob's] death for seventy days.   GENESIS 50:3

*G*rieving is a process that should not be denied or hurried. The rituals of wakes, visitations, funerals, and memorial services all help you move through stages of grief over the death of someone you love. If your loss is related to a friend's moving away, a damaged relationship, or the loss of a job, you still need to allow yourself to grieve in order to come to a point of healing after the loss.

Job stood up and tore his robe in grief [and said, " . . . The LORD gave me what I had, and the LORD has taken it away."   JOB 1:20-22

*L*osses always bring pain. Expressing that pain is not wrong or sinful; rather, it is a healthy expression of how God created you.

The thought of my suffering and homelessness is bitter beyond words. I will never forget this awful time, as I grieve over my loss. Yet I still dare to hope when I remember this: The faithful love of the LORD never ends! His mercies never cease. Great is his faithfulness; his mercies begin afresh each morning.

                                    LAMENTATIONS 3:18-25

*T*hose who know God grieve with the assurance of his love and have hope. Those who don't know God grieve alone and without hope.

You suffered along with those who were thrown into jail, and when all you owned was taken from you, you accepted it with joy. You knew there were better things waiting for you that will last forever.

HEBREWS 10:34

*I*t is important to allow yourself the necessary time to grieve, but there is a time for grieving to end. And as a Christian, you have the comfort of knowing that one day you will be with God in heaven, where all grief will be gone forever.

DIVINE PROMISE

THE LORD IS CLOSE TO THE BROKENHEARTED;
HE RESCUES THOSE WHOSE SPIRITS
ARE CRUSHED.   *Psalm 34:18*

Love

MY QUESTION *for* GOD

How can I show my love for God?

A Moment *with* God

No, O people, the LORD has told you what is good,
and this is what he requires of you: to do what
is right, to love mercy, and to walk humbly with
your God.   MICAH 6:8

[Jesus said,] "If you love me, obey my commandments."
JOHN 14:15

When you obey my commandments, you remain
in my love. . . . I have told you these things so that
you will be filled with my joy. Yes, your joy will
overflow!   JOHN 15:10-11

*O*bedience is one important way to express your love
for God. Just don't confuse that with trying to earn
God's love by doing good works. You obey God because you are *already* loved, not in order to be loved.
Your obedience will bring increasing joy because you
will see God at work in your life every day. What small
step of obedience can you take right now?

DIVINE PROMISE

IF YOU WILL OBEY ME AND KEEP MY COVENANT,
YOU WILL BE MY OWN SPECIAL TREASURE FROM
AMONG ALL THE PEOPLES ON EARTH; FOR ALL
THE EARTH BELONGS TO ME.   *Exodus 19:5*

Love

MY QUESTION for GOD

What are the qualities of true love?

A MOMENT with GOD

"It's not our custom here to marry off a younger daughter ahead of the firstborn," Laban replied. "But wait until the bridal week is over, then we'll give you Rachel, too—provided you promise to work another seven years for me." So Jacob agreed to work seven more years. A week after Jacob had married Leah, Laban gave him Rachel, too. (Laban gave Rachel a servant, Bilhah, to be her maid.) So Jacob slept with Rachel, too, and he loved her much more than Leah. He then stayed and worked for Laban the additional seven years.   GENESIS 29:26-30

Properly understood, love between a woman and a man is both a feeling and a commitment. It is a feeling of desire and devotion that draws two people together. It is a commitment to remain together no matter what happens to the feelings. True commitment, however, should enhance people's feelings for one another. Jacob demonstrated passion and commitment in agreeing to work another seven years for the woman he loved, despite the fact that he'd been tricked into marrying Leah. Jacob counted the additional years as immaterial compared to the value of his love for Rachel. Our culture often mistakes strong feelings, or even lust, for love, but the Bible reminds you that love is sealed by an act of commitment and faithfulness.

DIVINE PROMISE

LOVE IS PATIENT AND KIND. LOVE IS NOT
JEALOUS OR BOASTFUL OR PROUD OR RUDE.
IT DOES NOT DEMAND ITS OWN WAY. IT IS
NOT IRRITABLE, AND IT KEEPS NO RECORD
OF BEING WRONGED. IT DOES NOT REJOICE
ABOUT INJUSTICE BUT REJOICES WHENEVER
THE TRUTH WINS OUT. LOVE NEVER GIVES UP,
NEVER LOSES FAITH, IS ALWAYS HOPEFUL, AND
ENDURES THROUGH EVERY CIRCUMSTANCE.

1 Corinthians 13:4-7

Loyalty

MY QUESTION *for* GOD

How is loyalty an expression of true friendship?

A MOMENT *with* GOD

[The women] wept together, and Orpah kissed her mother-in-law good-bye. But Ruth clung tightly to Naomi. "Look," Naomi said to her, "your sister-in-law has gone back to her people and to her gods. You should do the same." But Ruth replied, "Don't ask me to leave you and turn back. Wherever you go, I will go; wherever you live, I will live. Your people will be my people, and your God will be my God."   RUTH 1:14-16

*R*uth's loyalty and commitment to her mother-in-law went beyond their cultural expectations. The two women had become friends. True friendship is characterized by loyalty, no matter what happens around you. There is a vast difference between knowing someone well and being a true friend. The greatest evidence of genuine friendship is loyalty, being available to help in times of distress or personal struggle. Too many people—and relatives!—are fair-weather friends. They stick around when the relationship benefits them, and they leave when they're not getting anything out of it. Think about your friends, and consider your loyalty to them. What can you do to become more loyal? True loyalty passes the test of adversity and brings a divine moment into the life of your friend.

DIVINE PROMISE

LOVE NEVER GIVES UP, NEVER LOSES FAITH, IS ALWAYS HOPEFUL, AND ENDURES THROUGH EVERY CIRCUMSTANCE.   *1 Corinthians 13:7*

Marriage

MY QUESTION *for* GOD

How does my marriage commitment reflect my commitment to God?

A MOMENT *with* GOD

As the Scriptures say, "A man leaves his father and mother and is joined to his wife, and the two are united into one." This is a great mystery, but it is an illustration of the way Christ and the church are one.

EPHESIANS 5:31-32

*M*arriage is frequently used as an illustration for the holy relationship between God and his people. Both relationships are formed on the basis of a covenant—a holy promise—to be faithful to one another exclusively. God insists on being the one divine love in your life—the one God whom you commit to loving, serving, and obeying as long as you live. The marriage union is symbolic of that commitment. As you commit to loving and serving your mate, you learn to better love and serve God. As you remain faithful to your mate, you understand more of what it means to be faithful to God. This faithfulness allows you to share an intimacy and a common purpose that is not possible in a casual relationship where there is little commitment.

DIVINE PROMISE

[JESUS SAID,] "SINCE THEY ARE NO LONGER TWO BUT ONE, LET NO ONE SPLIT APART WHAT GOD HAS JOINED TOGETHER." *Matthew 19:4-6*

Marriage

What are some keys to a happy, strong marriage?

[Joshua said,] "Choose today whom you will serve.
. . . But as for me and my family, we will serve the
LORD."   JOSHUA 24:15

Can two people walk together without agreeing on
the direction?   AMOS 3:3

A united purpose to serve the Lord is one key to a
strong marriage. If you want to take a walk with someone, you must decide together on the direction. If you
want to walk through life with your spouse, you must
decide together which direction you want to go—toward an eternal destination or away. This is the key to
experiencing daily divine moments together.

Rejoice in the wife of your youth. She is a loving deer,
a graceful doe. Let her breasts satisfy you always. May
you always be captivated by her love.   PROVERBS 5:18-19

*P*hysical faithfulness to your spouse is another necessary key to a strong and happy marriage. Without
faithfulness there is no real trust or intimacy.

[Jesus said,] "Since they are no longer two but one,
let no one split apart what God has joined together."

MATTHEW 19:4-6

*C*ommitment to staying together no matter what is essential for a strong and lasting relationship. If you leave open the option of splitting up someday, chances are you will. If you don't see breaking up as an option, you will remain committed to making your marriage work. This commitment joins you together in pursuing and accomplishing shared, lifelong goals.

We should help others do what is right and build them up in the Lord.   ROMANS 15:1-2

*S*elf-sacrifice is essential to a strong marriage. This means putting your spouse's needs and interests first. Who wouldn't want to be in a relationship where you are always meeting your spouse's needs before attending to your own?

May God . . . help you live in complete harmony with each other, as is fitting for followers of Christ Jesus. Then all of you can join together with one voice, giving praise and glory to God.   ROMANS 15:5-6

*L*earn to understand each other's differences and celebrate them. This fosters respect for each other and turns differences that would normally annoy or distract you into strengths that interest and help you.

Submit to one another out of reverence for Christ.

                                                   EPHESIANS 5:21

*M*utual submission in serving each other is a key to a strong marriage because it involves accountability, vulnerability, and confession.

Confess your sins to each other and pray for each other.   JAMES 5:16

*P*raying with and for each other helps to bond you together in marriage.

Our letters have been straightforward, and there is nothing written between the lines and nothing you can't understand. I hope someday you will fully understand us, even if you don't understand us now.

2 CORINTHIANS 1:13-14

*G*ood communication is a necessity. Since mind reading is possible only for God, talk to your spouse, and keep the lines of communication open, even when a conversation is awkward or hard. Instead of making each other guess, be honest. This will build trust and comfort into your relationship.

She brings [her husband] good, not harm, all the days of her life.   PROVERBS 31:12

*R*egular affirmation will enhance each other's value and build a strong marriage. Everyone needs to feel valued. Find ways to affirm your spouse each day, and you will build strength and joy in your marriage.

The husband should fulfill his wife's sexual needs, and the wife should fulfill her husband's needs.

1 CORINTHIANS 7:3

A healthy sex life is important for a strong and happy marriage because it allows you to express intimacy and vulnerability in a way different from any other relationship. It is a way you can share special closeness that demonstrates your complete openness to one another. This is what sets marriage apart as a relationship like no other and makes it a symbol of our relationship with God.

Love is patient and kind. Love is not jealous or boastful or proud or rude. It does not demand its own way. It is not irritable, and it keeps no record of being wronged.

1 CORINTHIANS 13:4-5

*E*xpressing unconditional love means doing the right thing even when your spouse does something that hurts you. Consistently demonstrating unconditional love is perhaps the hardest thing to do in a marriage, but it is the most effective way to have a great relationship and to win over the heart of even the most stubborn spouse.

DIVINE PROMISE

AS THE SCRIPTURES SAY, "A MAN LEAVES HIS FATHER AND MOTHER AND IS JOINED TO HIS WIFE, AND THE TWO ARE UNITED INTO ONE."

Ephesians 5:31

Meditation

MY QUESTION *for* GOD

How does meditation help my spiritual focus?

A MOMENT *with* GOD

I wait quietly before God, for my victory comes from him. . . . Let all that I am wait quietly before God, for my hope is in him.   PSALM 62:1, 5

I lie awake thinking of you, meditating on you through the night.   PSALM 63:6

I recall all you have done, O LORD; I remember your wonderful deeds of long ago. They are constantly in my thoughts. I cannot stop thinking about your mighty works.   PSALM 77:11-12

I remember the days of old. I ponder all your great works and think about what you have done. PSALM 143:5

I will meditate on your majestic, glorious splendor and your wonderful miracles.   PSALM 145:5

Meditation is setting aside time to intentionally think about God, talk to him, and listen to him. When we make the time to really listen to God, we remove ourselves from the distractions and noise of the world around us and move within range of his voice. We prepare ourselves to be teachable and to have our desires molded into what God desires. As a result, we change, and our thoughts and actions fall more in line with God's commands.

Meditation goes beyond the study of God to communion with him that ultimately leads to godly actions. Remember God first thing in the morning, and fall asleep with him on your mind. Meditate on God as the source of the hope you think you've lost. Think about him with a thankful heart when you have plenty, for you will need him when you have little. Meditate on him and his great love for you. Weave him into the fabric of your life so that your children and grandchildren will learn to love God with a grateful heart from their earliest days. Meditating on God and his Word will keep your spiritual walk strong and focused.

DIVINE PROMISE

YOU WILL KEEP IN PERFECT PEACE ALL WHO
TRUST IN YOU, ALL WHOSE THOUGHTS ARE
FIXED ON YOU! *Isaiah 26:3*

Mentoring

MY QUESTION *for* GOD

What are the blessings of encouraging godliness in younger generations?

A MOMENT *with* GOD

As for you, Titus, promote the kind of living that reflects wholesome teaching. Teach the older men to exercise self-control, to be worthy of respect, and to live wisely. They must have sound faith and

be filled with love and patience. Similarly, teach
the older women to live in a way that honors God.
They must not slander others or be heavy drinkers.
Instead, they should teach others what is good. These
older women must train the younger women to love
their husbands and their children, to live wisely and
be pure, to work in their homes, to do good, and to
be submissive to their husbands. Then they will not
bring shame on the word of God. In the same way,
encourage the young men to live wisely. And you
yourself must be an example to them by doing good
works of every kind. Let everything you do reflect
the integrity and seriousness of your teaching. Teach
the truth so that your teaching can't be criticized.
Then those who oppose us will be ashamed and have
nothing bad to say about us.   TITUS 2:1-8

A mentoring relationship has the specific purpose of
teaching and learning. Good mentors commit to building a relationship with someone younger or with less
life experience. Through this relationship, mentors
share wisdom, life experience, and support in hopes of
helping the ones they are mentoring to learn and grow.
Similarly, God sent the Holy Spirit as your spiritual
mentor. Through the Spirit, God helps you to build
a relationship with him and guides you into wisdom,
maturity, and understanding. Mentoring or being men-
tored is a powerful way to experience divine moments
because it requires you to spend time with another for
the purpose of learning about God.

DIVINE PROMISE

LET ME TEACH YOU, BECAUSE I AM HUMBLE
AND GENTLE AT HEART, AND YOU WILL FIND
REST FOR YOUR SOULS.   *Matthew 11:29*

Mercy

MY QUESTION *for* GOD

How does God's mercy affect my daily life?

A MOMENT *with* GOD

The LORD is compassionate and merciful, slow to get
angry and filled with unfailing love.   PSALM 103:8

*M*ercy is another word for the amazing kindness
God showers on us in not treating us as our sins deserve. God's greatest act of mercy is the offer of salvation and eternal life, even though at times we have
ignored him, neglected him, and rebelled against him.
God's mercy sets you free from the power of sin when
he forgives you, so that you can choose each day to fight
your sinful nature. God's mercy changes your life because you understand what it feels like to be loved even
when you have not loved in return. This should cause
you to love others in the same way that God loves you,
creating in their lives a divine moment. To whom can
you be an example of God's mercy today?

DIVINE PROMISE

[THE LORD] DOES NOT PUNISH US FOR ALL OUR
SINS; HE DOES NOT DEAL HARSHLY WITH US, AS
WE DESERVE.   *Psalm 103:10*

Miracles

MY QUESTIONS *for* GOD

*Does God still perform miracles today? How can I see more
miracles in my life?*

A MOMENT *with* GOD

Moses and Aaron did just as the LORD had
commanded them. When Aaron raised his hand and
struck the ground with his staff, gnats infested the
entire land, covering the Egyptians and their animals.
All the dust in the land of Egypt turned into gnats.
Pharaoh's magicians tried to do the same thing with
their secret arts, but this time they failed. And the
gnats covered everyone, people and animals alike.
"This is the finger of God!" the magicians exclaimed
to Pharaoh. But Pharaoh's heart remained hard.
He wouldn't listen to them, just as the Lord had
predicted.   EXODUS 8:17-19

Come and see what our God has done, what awesome
miracles he performs for people!   PSALM 66:5

God confirmed the message by giving signs and
wonders and various miracles and gifts of the Holy
Spirit whenever he chose.   HEBREWS 2:4

The miracles of God recorded in the Bible can seem like ancient myths if you fail to recognize God's intervention in your life today. Just as Pharaoh was blind to the miracles God performed right before his eyes, you, too, can blind yourself to God's miracles and fail to notice the mighty work God is doing all around you. Maybe you think a miracle is always a dramatic event such as raising a dead person to life. But miracles are happening all around you. These supernatural occurrences may not be as dramatic as the parting of the Red Sea, but they are no less powerful. The birth of a baby, an awesome sunset, the healing of an illness, the restoration of a hopeless relationship, the rebirth of the earth in spring, salvation by faith alone, the specific call of God in your life. These are just a few. If you think you've never seen a miracle, look closer. They are happening all around you.

DIVINE PROMISE

NO PAGAN GOD IS LIKE YOU, O LORD. NONE CAN DO WHAT YOU DO! *Psalm 86:8*

Mistakes

MY QUESTION *for* GOD

I make so many mistakes. Is there any hope that God can still use me?

A MOMENT *with* GOD

[Jesus said,] "Simon, Simon, Satan has asked to sift each of you like wheat. But I have pleaded in prayer for you, Simon, that your faith should not fail. So when you have repented and turned to me again, strengthen your brothers."   LUKE 22:31-32

Jesus said, "Peter, let me tell you something. Before the rooster crows tomorrow morning, you will deny three times that you even know me."   LUKE 22:34

𝒦nowing that Simon Peter was heading for disaster, Jesus prayed for him, making two requests of his heavenly Father: first, that Peter's mistakes would not cause him to lose his faith, and second, that Peter would eventually use the lessons he learned from his error to strengthen others spiritually. Jesus' prayers were answered. Peter went on to become the leader of the first church in Jerusalem and an encourager of those who were suffering for their faith.

Nothing about your life is useless to God—but that does not give you an excuse for sinning. The heartache and consequences of sin can continue for a lifetime—even to future generations. Yet the wonder of grace is that God can use your worst failures to strengthen your faith and enable you to better comfort and help others.

DIVINE PROMISE

THE LORD DIRECTS THE STEPS OF THE GODLY.
HE DELIGHTS IN EVERY DETAIL OF THEIR
LIVES. THOUGH THEY STUMBLE, THEY WILL
NEVER FALL, FOR THE LORD HOLDS THEM BY
THE HAND.   *Psalm 37:23-24*

Mystery

MY QUESTION *for* GOD

*Why is it important that there are mysteries about God we'll
never know?*

A MOMENT *with* GOD

The LORD our God has secrets known to no one.
We are not accountable for them, but we and our
children are accountable forever for all that he has
revealed to us, so that we may obey all the terms of
these instructions.   DEUTERONOMY 29:29

Just as you cannot understand the path of the wind
or the mystery of a tiny baby growing in its mother's
womb, so you cannot understand the activity of God,
who does all things.   ECCLESIASTES 11:5

Dear friends, we are already God's children, but
he has not yet shown us what we will be like when
Christ appears. But we do know that we will be like
him, for we will see him as he really is.   1 JOHN 3:2

*I*f God's nature and knowledge could be totally known by humans, God would cease to be a God who inspires our awe. God's mysteries are opportunities for faith. If you knew everything there was to know about God or his plans for your life, there would be no need for faith. God has given you all you need to know in order to believe in him. Continue to pursue learning all that God has already revealed about himself, and you will discover him in new and exciting ways. You are not responsible for the mysteries about God that you cannot know, but you are responsible for what you can know about him. Following him is a lifelong adventure of discovery.

DIVINE PROMISE

TRULY, O GOD OF ISRAEL, OUR SAVIOR, YOU
WORK IN MYSTERIOUS WAYS.   *Isaiah 45:15*

Needs

MY QUESTION *for* GOD

How does depending on God for my needs bring contentment?

A MOMENT *with* GOD

Fear the LORD, you his godly people, for those who fear him will have all they need.   PSALM 34:9

Your Father knows exactly what you need even before you ask him!   MATTHEW 6:8

God will generously provide all you need. Then you
will always have everything you need and plenty left
over to share with others.   2 CORINTHIANS 9:8

If we have enough food and clothing, let us be content.
                                        1 TIMOTHY 6:8

Don't love money; be satisfied with what you have.
For God has said, "I will never fail you. I will never
abandon you."   HEBREWS 13:5

In order to survive and thrive, all people have basic
needs: food, water, shelter, and love. Needs are different from "wants"; when your needs are met, you can
be content and satisfied. Wants, even when fulfilled,
often leave you unsatisfied, discontented, and looking
for more. Wants are not always negative, but when they
oppose God's desires, they become fuel for the fires of
jealousy, covetousness, deceit, materialism, or other
sins that result when you become obsessed with getting what you want. Your needs allow God to show his
power and provision for you and to teach you that he
is sufficient. Learning to recognize the difference between needs and wants allows you to find contentment
in living God's way. The more you focus on what the
Lord values, the more you will be able to distinguish
your needs from your wants. If you often feel discontented, you may be focusing more on what you want
than on what God knows you need.

DIVINE PROMISE

THE LORD IS MY SHEPHERD; I HAVE ALL THAT I NEED.   *Psalm 23:1*

Neglect

MY QUESTION *for* GOD

In what ways do I neglect God?

A MOMENT *with* GOD

This is what the LORD of Heaven's Armies says: The people are saying, "The time has not yet come to rebuild the house of the LORD." Then the LORD sent this message through the prophet Haggai: "Why are you living in luxurious houses while my house lies in ruins? This is what the LORD of Heaven's Armies says: Look at what's happening to you! You have planted much but harvest little. You eat but are not satisfied. You drink but are still thirsty. You put on clothes but cannot keep warm. Your wages disappear as though you were putting them in pockets filled with holes!"

HAGGAI 1:2-6

What good is it, dear brothers and sisters, if you say you have faith but don't show it by your actions? Can that kind of faith save anyone?

JAMES 2:14

The exiles returning to their homeland of Israel never said that rebuilding the Temple wasn't important. They just protested that it wasn't the right time for it yet. But God condemned them for taking care of themselves while allowing his house to remain a pile of rubble. The issue wasn't timing; it was priority. We often use the same excuse, claiming that it doesn't feel like the right time to start the practice of daily Bible study, to begin tithing, to share the gospel with a non-Christian friend, or to stop a sinful habit. Yet few of us would say it doesn't feel like the right time to pick up our paychecks! Any excuse for neglecting our basic Christian duty is merely a cloak for a fearful spirit or a stubborn heart. When you make God your top priority, you will experience divine moments where you can see his active work and blessing in your life.

DIVINE PROMISE

SEEK THE KINGDOM OF GOD ABOVE ALL ELSE, AND LIVE RIGHTEOUSLY, AND HE WILL GIVE YOU EVERYTHING YOU NEED. *Matthew 6:33*

Neighbors

MY QUESTION *for* GOD

How can I recognize opportunities to share God's love with my neighbors?

A MOMENT *with* GOD

The man wanted to justify his actions, so he asked Jesus, "And who is my neighbor?" Jesus replied with a story: "A Jewish man was traveling on a trip from Jerusalem to Jericho, and he was attacked by bandits. They stripped him of his clothes, beat him up, and left him half dead beside the road. By chance a priest came along. . . . and passed him by. A Temple assistant walked over and looked at him lying there, but he also passed by on the other side. "Then a despised Samaritan came along, and when he saw the man, he felt compassion for him. Going over to him, the Samaritan soothed his wounds with olive oil and wine and bandaged them. Then he put the man on his own donkey and took him to an inn, where he took care of him. The next day he handed the innkeeper two silver coins, telling him, 'Take care of this man. If his bill runs higher than this, I'll pay you the next time I'm here.' "Now which of these three would you say was a neighbor to the man who was attacked by bandits?" Jesus asked. The man replied, "The one who showed him mercy." Then Jesus said, "Yes, now go and do the same."   LUKE 10:29-37

Most of us think of our neighbors as the people who live next door or across the street. Jesus' teachings expand your neighborhood to involve anyone around you who needs his love and care. This means that the person next to you on the plane, your coworkers, or the homeless in your town are also your neighbors. It is also important to expand your neighborhood to people around the world who need the love of Christ. When you begin to view people you meet or hear about as your neighbors, you will see these encounters as divine

moments that allow you to share the love of Christ.
What neighbors have come across your path today?

DIVINE PROMISE

IT IS GOOD WHEN YOU OBEY THE ROYAL LAW
AS FOUND IN THE SCRIPTURES: "LOVE YOUR
NEIGHBOR AS YOURSELF." *James 2:8*

Obedience

MY QUESTION *for* GOD

How can I be inspired to want to obey God?

A MOMENT *with* GOD

If you love me, obey my commandments.   JOHN 14:15

Dear friends, you always followed my instructions
when I was with you. And now that I am away, it is
even more important. Work hard to show the results
of your salvation, obeying God with deep reverence
and fear.   PHILIPPIANS 2:12

*O*nce you have experienced God's love and work in
your life, you will want to show your appreciation and
gratitude by obeying him. Obedience is the visible expression of your love.

Do what is right and good in the LORD's sight, so all
will go well with you.   DEUTERONOMY 6:18

*T*he right thing to do is the smart thing to do. God's commandments are not burdensome obligations but pathways to joyful, meaningful, and satisfying lives. God's call to obedience comes from his own commitment to your well-being. Since God is the creator of life, he knows the best way to live. Obedience demonstrates your willingness to accept what God says and trust that his way is best for you.

DIVINE PROMISE

GOD IS WORKING IN YOU, GIVING YOU THE DESIRE AND THE POWER TO DO WHAT PLEASES HIM. *Philippians 2:13*

Opportunities

MY QUESTION *for* GOD

How do I make the most of the opportunities that come my way?

A MOMENT *with* GOD

A hard worker has plenty of food, but a person who chases fantasies has no sense. PROVERBS 12:11

I will be staying here at Ephesus until the Festival of Pentecost. There is a wide-open door for a great work here, although many oppose me.

1 CORINTHIANS 16:8-9

Make the most of every opportunity in these evil days.

EPHESIANS 5:16

$\mathscr{I}$n many ways our lives are defined by opportunities seized or missed. According to the Bible, we are to take advantage of opportunities by responding with bold action when we recognize them as God-given chances to participate in his purpose. We must be prepared at all times to recognize and act on the opportunities that God creates for us to be used by and for him. When you believe that God is presenting you with an opportunity, respond quickly, and work hard to maximize what God has put before you. Be willing to change your plans in order to take advantage of a God-given opportunity. You will be motivated when you think of how God might use you because you've made yourself available for his work. Keep your eyes open for what God will bring your way.

DIVINE PROMISE

WE MUST QUICKLY CARRY OUT THE TASKS
ASSIGNED US BY THE ONE WHO SENT US.
THE NIGHT IS COMING, AND THEN NO ONE
CAN WORK.   *John 9:4*

Overcoming

MY QUESTION *for* GOD

Will God help me escape life's troubles?

A MOMENT *with* GOD

Jesus, full of the Holy Spirit, returned from the Jordan
River. He was led by the Spirit in the wilderness,
where he was tempted by the devil for forty days. Jesus
ate nothing all that time and became very hungry.

LUKE 4:1-2

*O*verwhelmed. Defeated. Powerless. Out of control.
You may sometimes feel as if there's no way to overcome your circumstances or struggles. Life will present
immense obstacles and invincible opponents, and God
does not promise to help you escape. But take heart!
The ability to overcome is the birthright of believers.
And God has given you his Holy Spirit to help you overcome the obstacles and temptations in your life.

But the fact that you have God's presence with you
doesn't mean that you won't struggle. Being filled with
the Holy Spirit did not prevent Jesus from being tempted,
but it did help him overcome temptation. As long as you
live on this earth, you will never be free from trouble,
but you can have the power to overcome it through the
Holy Spirit's help. When you begin to see the obstacles
in your life as opportunities for God to show his power,
they will not seem so overwhelming. The very hardships
and weaknesses that frighten you may be the tools God
wants to use to help you overcome.

THE RIGHTEOUS KEEP MOVING FORWARD,
AND THOSE WITH CLEAN HANDS BECOME
STRONGER AND STRONGER.   *Job 17:9*

Overwhelmed

My Question *for* God

What can I do when I feel overwhelmed?

A Moment *with* God

Five of you will chase a hundred, and a hundred of
you will chase ten thousand! All your enemies will
fall beneath your sword.   Leviticus 26:8

Each one of you will put to flight a thousand of the
enemy, for the Lord your God fights for you, just as
he has promised.   Joshua 23:10

*B*e encouraged that the power of God is for you, regardless of the number of enemies against you. God
used David to overcome Goliath. He used Gideon's
three hundred soldiers to defeat the vast armies of
Midian. And he used twelve disciples to establish the
worldwide church. Knowing that God works through
your weaknesses and limitations can be a great encouragement. You don't have to be smart or strong or beautiful for God to do great things through you. You need
only to be obedient.

We also pray that you will be strengthened with all his glorious power so you will have all the endurance and patience you need. May you be filled with joy, always thanking the Father. He has enabled you to share in the inheritance that belongs to his people, who live in the light. For he has rescued us from the kingdom of darkness and transferred us into the Kingdom of his dear Son, who purchased our freedom and forgave our sins.   COLOSSIANS 1:11-14

*B*e encouraged that you have been rescued from sin's control and Satan's power. God, through the power of his Holy Spirit, has given you all you need to overcome whatever overwhelms you. When you remember that you are already free from sin's deadly power, the problems of this world lose much of their grip on you.

DIVINE PROMISE

GOD IS OUR REFUGE AND STRENGTH, ALWAYS READY TO HELP IN TIMES OF TROUBLE.   *Psalm 46:1*

Pain

MY QUESTION *for* GOD

What hope do I have for living through painful circumstances?

A Moment *with* God

We believers also groan, even though we have the Holy Spirit within us as a foretaste of future glory, for we long for our bodies to be released from sin and suffering. We, too, wait with eager hope for the day when God will give us our full rights as his adopted children, including the new bodies he has promised us. We were given this hope when we were saved.

ROMANS 8:23-24

After you have suffered a little while, he will restore, support, and strengthen you, and he will place you on a firm foundation.   1 PETER 5:10

Whether from betrayal, neglect, or abandonment or from a broken bone or failing health—the result is some kind of emotional or physical pain. When you look back on your life, you may remember the physical tension of your aching body or the chest-tightening ache that comes from a broken heart. Your greatest hope in times of pain is finding healing from God. He doesn't take the day off and forget about you. When you accidentally cut yourself, you become completely focused on how bad it is and on how to stop the bleeding. When you feel God has abandoned you, it might be because you have become so focused on easing the pain of your problems that you have neglected God and forgotten that he has promised to help you in your difficulties. Although God does not promise to remove your pain in this life, he does promise to be with you in it and give you hope and purpose in midst of your aching body and souls.

DIVINE PROMISE

WHAT WE SUFFER NOW IS NOTHING
COMPARED TO THE GLORY HE WILL REVEAL
TO US LATER.   *Romans 8:18*

Passion

MY QUESTION *for* GOD

Why can't I always be on fire for God?

A MOMENT *with* GOD

Besides Pharaoh's daughter, [King Solomon] married women from Moab, Ammon, Edom, Sidon, and from among the Hittites. The LORD had clearly instructed the people of Israel, "You must not marry them, because they will turn your hearts to their gods." Yet Solomon insisted on loving them anyway. . . . And in fact, they did turn his heart away from the LORD.

1 KINGS 11:1-3

When sin gets a foothold in your life, it always leads you away from God and produces an apathetic attitude towards him. Satan will use all his power to keep you from getting excited about following God.

The woman was convinced. She saw that the tree
was beautiful and its fruit looked delicious, and she
wanted the wisdom it would give her. So she took
some of the fruit and ate it. Then she gave some to
her husband, who was with her, and he ate it, too.

GENESIS 3:6

*T*emptation takes your focus off God and makes it
more exciting to think about something else. When
this happens, it's not that you really want to move
away from God, but something else has suddenly got
your attention! If what you're excited about is not what
God wants you to do, your passion for God will quickly
die.

[Jesus said,] "Stay here and keep watch with me."
He went on a little farther and fell to the ground.
He prayed that, if it were possible, the awful hour
awaiting him might pass him by. "Abba, Father," he
cried out, "everything is possible for you. Please take
this cup of suffering away from me. Yet I want your
will to be done, not mine." Then he returned and
found the disciples asleep. He said to Peter, "Simon,
are you asleep? Couldn't you watch with me even
one hour? Keep watch and pray, so that you will not
give in to temptation. For the spirit is willing, but the
body is weak."

MARK 14:32-38

*S*ometimes you're just too tired, or you just don't see
the significance of what is going on around you. Peter

thought this was just another night out. If he'd had his
spiritual antenna up, he might have sensed how significant this night was going to be. We must be passionate
about looking for God in every circumstance.

You must continue to believe this truth and stand
firmly in it. Don't drift away from the assurance
you received when you heard the Good News. The
Good News has been preached all over the world,
and I, Paul, have been appointed as God's servant to
proclaim it.   COLOSSIANS 1:23

We must listen very carefully to the truth we have
heard, or we may drift away from it.   HEBREWS 2:1

[The Lord said,] "I have this complaint against you.
You don't love me or each other as you did at first!"

REVELATION 2:4

$\mathcal{L}$ike all relationships, your relationship with God
takes effort and energy. God continues to be fully
committed to you. In order for your relationship to
continue to be exciting, you must be fully committed
to him—diligent in your efforts to know him better.
Three things can really make a difference: consistent
study of God's Word, a thankful heart, and acts of
service toward others. These will fight off feelings of
apathy toward God and will reignite your passion for
him and his purpose for you.

DIVINE PROMISE

[GOD SAID,] "I WILL GIVE THEM SINGLENESS
OF HEART AND PUT A NEW SPIRIT WITHIN
THEM. I WILL TAKE AWAY THEIR STONY,
STUBBORN HEART AND GIVE THEM A TENDER,
RESPONSIVE HEART." *Ezekiel 11:19*

Past

MY QUESTION *for* GOD

Can I live a healthy, godly life, in spite of my past?

A MOMENT *with* GOD

I remember the days of old. I ponder all your great
works and think about what you have done. PSALM 143:5

[The Lord said,] "Though your sins are like scarlet,
I will make them as white as snow. Though they are
red like crimson, I will make them as white as wool."

ISAIAH 1:18

You know what I was like when I followed the Jewish
religion—how I violently persecuted God's church. I
did my best to destroy it.   GALATIANS 1:13

I focus on this one thing: Forgetting the past and
looking forward to what lies ahead.   PHILIPPIANS 3:13

*Y*our memory of the past is like a photo album that
contains snapshots of your life. These snapshots are not
just of happy moments and celebrations; they also re-

cord your failures, tragedies, and acts that caused you deep shame. Most of us would like to lock some of our past away or tear out the snapshots that expose the parts we'd like to forget. The apostle Paul, considered one of the great leaders in the New Testament, had a past he wished he could forget. His memory album was full of snapshots from his days of persecuting and killing Christians. What an immense burden of regret he could have carried. But Paul understood that his past had been redeemed through God's healing and forgiveness.

How you view your past will affect how you live in the present and the future. Some of us have good pasts with a strong spiritual heritage from loving parents and mentors. Don't take that for granted; use it to help others. Some of us have pasts filled with regrets for actions that were wrong and hurtful. No matter what you've done, God is ready to forgive you, cleanse you on the inside, and give you a fresh start—fully forgiven. Some people been victims of abuse, neglect, violence, and shameful acts. This is the most difficult past to deal with. But God wants to redeem your past and restore you—you just need to ask him. He can remove your regret, guilt, and shame and free you to live in peace with purpose and joy.

DIVINE PROMISE

[GOD SAID,] "FEAR NOT; YOU WILL NO LONGER
LIVE IN SHAME. DON'T BE AFRAID; THERE
IS NO MORE DISGRACE FOR YOU. YOU WILL
NO LONGER REMEMBER THE SHAME OF
YOUR YOUTH." *Isaiah 54:4*

Patience

MY QUESTION for GOD

How can I learn patience?

A MOMENT with GOD

The Holy Spirit produces this kind of fruit in our
lives: love, joy, peace, patience.   GALATIANS 5:22

Contrary to popular opinion, patience is not merely
a personality trait. It is a by-product of the presence
and work of God in your heart. Achieving worthwhile
goals is rarely accomplished in a quantum leap. Learning to be more patient comes from taking small, faithful steps day by day.

Because of his glory and excellence, he has given us
great and precious promises. These are the promises
that enable you to share his divine nature and escape
the world's corruption caused by human desires.
In view of all this, make every effort to respond
to God's promises. Supplement your faith with a
generous provision of moral excellence, and moral
excellence with knowledge, and knowledge with self-
control, and self-control with patient endurance, and
patient endurance with godliness, and godliness with
brotherly affection, and brotherly affection with love
for everyone.   2 PETER 1:4-7

$\mathcal{P}$atience comes through perseverance and endurance, and it allows you to respond to frustrating circumstances with grace and self-control.

I waited patiently for the LORD to help me, and he turned to me and heard my cry.   PSALM 40:1

$\mathcal{P}$atience comes from having a solid hope in God's plans, especially his eternal plans for you. When you know that your long-range future is settled and secure, you can be more patient during today's frustrations.

Consider the farmers who patiently wait for the rains in the fall and in the spring. They eagerly look for the valuable harvest to ripen.   JAMES 5:7-8

$\mathcal{W}$hether you're waiting for crops to ripen, a traffic jam to unsnarl, a child to mature, or God to perfect you, you can grow in patience by recognizing that these things take time and that there is very little you can do to speed them up. A key to understanding God's will is to understand God's timing.

DIVINE PROMISE

PATIENT ENDURANCE IS WHAT YOU NEED NOW, SO THAT YOU WILL CONTINUE TO DO GOD'S WILL. THEN YOU WILL RECEIVE ALL THAT HE HAS PROMISED.   *Hebrews 10:36*

Peace

MY QUESTION *for* GOD

Can I have peace in a world that is anything but peaceful?

A MOMENT *with* GOD

You will keep in perfect peace all who trust in you,
all whose thoughts are fixed on you!   ISAIAH 26:3

[Jesus said,] "I am leaving you with a gift—peace
of mind and heart. And the peace I give is a gift the
world cannot give. So don't be troubled or afraid.
Remember what I told you: I am going away, but I
will come back to you again. If you really loved me,
you would be happy that I am going to the Father,
who is greater than I am."   JOHN 14:27-28

So many things affect peace—conflict, uncertainty,
busyness, worry, fear. How can you have peace with
all that? You can't prevent many of these things from
invading your life, but you can have peace—a quiet,
unshakable confidence—about the outcome. How do
some people have such amazing peace just before they
are martyred for their faith in Jesus? They know where
they are going and that their treasure is in heaven. Let
that assurance keep you from panicking in today's
storms. The outcome is certain.

DIVINE PROMISE

[JESUS SAID,] "DON'T LET YOUR HEARTS BE
TROUBLED. TRUST IN GOD, AND TRUST ALSO
IN ME. THERE IS MORE THAN ENOUGH ROOM
IN MY FATHER'S HOME. IF THIS WERE NOT
SO, WOULD I HAVE TOLD YOU THAT I AM
GOING TO PREPARE A PLACE FOR YOU? WHEN
EVERYTHING IS READY, I WILL COME AND GET
YOU, SO THAT YOU WILL ALWAYS BE WITH ME
WHERE I AM." *John 14:1-4*

Perseverance

MY QUESTION *for* GOD

*Life has pretty much just beaten me down. Can I really come
through struggles a stronger woman?*

A MOMENT *with* GOD

We think you ought to know, dear brothers and
sisters, about the trouble we went through in the
province of Asia. We were crushed and overwhelmed
beyond our ability to endure, and we thought we
would never live through it. In fact, we expected to
die. But as a result, we stopped relying on ourselves
and learned to rely only on God, who raises the dead.

2 CORINTHIANS 1:8-9

May the Lord lead your hearts into a full
understanding and expression of the love of God and
the patient endurance that comes from Christ.

2 THESSALONIANS 3:5

Dear brothers and sisters, when troubles come your way, consider it an opportunity for great joy. For you know that when your faith is tested, your endurance has a chance to grow. So let it grow, for when your endurance is fully developed, you will be perfect and complete, needing nothing.   JAMES 1:2-4

*P*erseverance has been well-defined as "courage stretched out." Although God sometimes delivers his people from difficult or painful circumstances, he often calls you to a courageous and enduring faithfulness in the middle of trials. Perseverance, according to the Bible, is not only enduring difficult situations but overcoming them with obedience, hope, and joy. If you don't learn to persevere through your struggles, you will simply give up. But when you persevere until you come out the other side, you grow stronger in faith, you see the benefits of obedience to God, and you develop greater confidence that when problems strike again you can get through them.

DIVINE PROMISE

THE SOVEREIGN LORD IS MY STRENGTH! HE MAKES ME AS SUREFOOTED AS A DEER, ABLE TO TREAD UPON THE HEIGHTS. *Habakkuk 3:19*

Perspective

MY QUESTIONS *for* GOD

*How do I understand all the random circumstances that seem
to be coming my way? Is God really in charge or does a lot
just happen by chance?*

A MOMENT *with* GOD

The LORD will work out his plans for my life.

PSALM 138:8

I am Joseph, your brother, whom you sold into
slavery in Egypt. But don't be upset, and don't be
angry with yourselves for selling me to this place.
It was God who sent me here ahead of you to
preserve your lives. . . . It was God who sent me
here, not you!

GENESIS 45:4-5, 8

From our human perspective, the world and our individual lives often seem to be random and unpredictable, but God is still in control. Joseph's story shows
how God used even the unjust treatment of Joseph by
his own brothers to fulfill a bigger plan. People's sinful
ways do not ruin God's sovereign plans. In the end,
you will discover that your life is like a tapestry; right
now you can see only sections of the back, with all its
knots and loose ends. Someday you will see the front
in its beautiful entirety, the picture of world history
and your personal history from God's perspective. If
you can see unexpected and even unwelcome circumstances in this way, you'll embrace both the good and

the bad, knowing that through them, God is weaving a beautiful picture with your life.

DIVINE PROMISE

YOU SEE ME WHEN I TRAVEL AND WHEN I REST AT HOME. YOU KNOW EVERYTHING I DO.

Psalm 139:3

Perspective

MY QUESTION *for* GOD

What happens when I lose sight of God?

A MOMENT *with* GOD

The people of Israel said to Moses, "Look, we are doomed! We are dead! We are ruined! Everyone who even comes close to the Tabernacle of the LORD dies. Are we all doomed to die?"   NUMBERS 17:12-13

Martha was distracted by the big dinner she was preparing. She came to Jesus and said, "Lord, doesn't it seem unfair to you that my sister just sits here while I do all the work? Tell her to come and help me." But the Lord said to her, "My dear Martha, you are worried and upset over all these details!"   LUKE 10:40-41

*T*he perspective of the Israelites was completely opposite of reality. Instead of seeing the Tabernacle as a place to worship God, they saw it as a place to fear him. What happened? Their perspective of God changed because they began to choose disobedience over obedience and thus set themselves up for the natural and painful consequences of sin. Obeying God is the only way to keep an accurate perspective on life, because obedience keeps you focused on what is really important, leads you into God's will, and gives you an eternal orientation that affects the way you live here on earth. Obeying God shows you that all you really need is what God supplies in great abundance. When you drift away from consistent obedience to God, you lose your perspective. Your daily choices become more selfish, and you slide toward cynicism and dissatisfaction. But if you make God your first priority of the day, he will give you perspective on your activities for the rest of the day and a greater desire to obey him as you see the rewards of obedience. Ask God to show you what is really worth being concerned about, and you will maintain a right perspective.

DIVINE PROMISE

IF YOU TRY TO HANG ON TO YOUR LIFE, YOU WILL LOSE IT. BUT IF YOU GIVE UP YOUR LIFE FOR MY SAKE, YOU WILL SAVE IT. *Matthew 16:25*

Pleasure

MY QUESTION *for* GOD

Does it please God when we enjoy the things he's given us?

A MOMENT *with* GOD

I decided there is nothing better than to enjoy food
and drink and to find satisfaction in work. Then
I realized that these pleasures are from the hand
of God.   ECCLESIASTES 2:24

Since everything God created is good, we should
not reject any of it but receive it with thanks. For
we know it is made acceptable by the word of God
and prayer.   1 TIMOTHY 4:4-5

God intends for you to enjoy the good things he created for all people. When you are enjoying God's blessings, you are accepting his gifts to you, and he is pleased
when you use and bask in his special gifts to you.

Nehemiah continued, "Go and celebrate with a feast
of rich foods and sweet drinks, and share gifts of food
with people who have nothing prepared. This is a
sacred day before our LORD."   NEHEMIAH 8:10

It is good to enjoy occasions of celebrating God's
goodness and love. God is always pleased when you
gather with others in thankful celebration and the en-
joyment of food, friends, and blessings!

Jesus explained: "My nourishment comes from doing the will of God, who sent me, and from finishing his work."

JOHN 4:34

The best kind of pleasure is delighting in doing what God wants. This is most pleasing to God, who always wants what is best for you. When you find pleasure in obedience, you are enjoying life as God intended you to enjoy it—to the fullest!

DIVINE PROMISE

YOU HAVE GIVEN ME GREATER JOY THAN THOSE WHO HAVE ABUNDANT HARVESTS OF GRAIN AND NEW WINE. *Psalm 4:7*

Power of God

MY QUESTION *for* GOD

How can others see the power of God in me?

A MOMENT *with* GOD

Has the LORD redeemed you? Then speak out! Tell others he has redeemed you from your enemies.

PSALM 107:2

It is not that we think we are qualified to do anything on our own. Our qualification comes from God.

2 CORINTHIANS 3:5

God has not given us a spirit of fear and timidity, but
of power, love, and self-discipline.   2 TIMOTHY 1:7

*T*he same God who can instantly calm the storm on the
Sea of Galilee has the power to calm the storms in your
heart, dry up a flood of fear, quench a lust for sin, and
control the whirlwind of life. Those who have seen and
experienced God's miracles and his work in their hearts
have a great responsibility to tell their stories to others. Whether by God's power you have had a dramatic
life change or a quiet, steady walk of faith, your life is
a living demonstration of God's powerful work within
you. Use every opportunity to tell others your story of
God's work in you. How else will those who have not yet
experienced the power of God know what kind of God
lives in you and works through his people?

DIVINE PROMISE

[JESUS SAID,] "YOU WILL RECEIVE POWER WHEN
THE HOLY SPIRIT COMES UPON YOU. AND
YOU WILL BE MY WITNESSES, TELLING PEOPLE
ABOUT ME EVERYWHERE . . . TO THE ENDS OF
THE EARTH." *Acts 1:8*

Praise

MY QUESTION *for* GOD

*How can praise become a natural response to the presence of
God in my life?*

A Moment *with* God

Great is the LORD! He is most worthy of praise! He is to be feared above all gods. The gods of other nations are mere idols, but the LORD made the heavens!

1 CHRONICLES 16:25-26

Who can list the glorious miracles of the LORD? Who can ever praise him enough? PSALM 106:2

[Jesus] replied, "If they kept quiet, the stones along the road would burst into cheers!" LUKE 19:40

*P*raise is creation's natural response to the greatness of the Creator. It is not unusual for people to burst into spontaneous applause or cheers when a head of state or a celebrity enters a room, and your natural response when you enter God's presence through worship should be praise. The Bible teaches that God created the universe and provides for your needs; he alone is worthy of your highest praise. When you consider who God is and what he has done for you, praise is the only possible response. Jesus said that if people didn't lift their voices in praise, the very rocks and stones would cry out in praise to him!

DIVINE PROMISE

WHEN HE COMES ON THAT DAY, HE WILL RECEIVE GLORY FROM HIS HOLY PEOPLE—PRAISE FROM ALL WHO BELIEVE. AND THIS INCLUDES YOU, FOR YOU BELIEVED WHAT WE TOLD YOU ABOUT HIM. *2 Thessalonians 1:10*

Prayer

MY QUESTION *for* GOD

How do I talk to God?

A MOMENT *with* GOD

I will praise you, LORD, with all my heart.   PSALM 9:1

I confess my sins; I am deeply sorry for what I
have done.   PSALM 38:18

[Jesus said,] "Keep on asking, and you will receive
what you ask for. Keep on seeking, and you will find.
Keep on knocking, and the door will be opened to
you. For everyone who asks, receives. Everyone who
seeks, finds. And to everyone who knocks, the door
will be opened. You parents—if your children ask
for a loaf of bread, do you give them a stone instead?
Or if they ask for a fish, do you give them a snake?
Of course not! So if you sinful people know how to
give good gifts to your children, how much more will
your heavenly Father give good gifts to those who
ask him."   MATTHEW 7:7-11

*P*rayer is talking to God. As you talk to him, you
praise and thank him, confess sins, make requests,
express pain and frustration, and share what is happening in your life. Good conversation also includes
listening, so make time for God's Spirit to speak to
you. When you listen to God, he can make his wisdom
and resources available to you. Prayer can also soften

your heart and help you avoid the debilitating effects of anger, resentment, and bitterness. There's so much more to prayer than just getting an answer to a question or a solution for a problem. God often does more in your heart through your act of praying than he does in actually answering your prayer. As you persist in talking and listening, you will gain greater understanding of yourself, your situation, your motivation, God's nature, and his direction for your life.

DIVINE PROMISE

DON'T WORRY ABOUT ANYTHING; INSTEAD, PRAY ABOUT EVERYTHING. TELL GOD WHAT YOU NEED, AND THANK HIM FOR ALL HE HAS DONE. THEN YOU WILL EXPERIENCE GOD'S PEACE, WHICH EXCEEDS ANYTHING WE CAN UNDERSTAND. HIS PEACE WILL GUARD YOUR HEARTS AND MINDS AS YOU LIVE IN CHRIST JESUS. *Philippians 4:6-7*

Prayer

MY QUESTION *for* GOD

Does God always answer prayer?

A MOMENT *with* GOD

I love the LORD because he hears my voice and my prayer for mercy. PSALM 116:1

Three different times I begged the Lord to take it
away. Each time he said, " . . . My power works best
in weakness." So now I am glad to boast about my
weaknesses, so that the power of Christ can work
through me.   2 CORINTHIANS 12:8-9

God listens carefully to every prayer and answers it.
His answer may be yes, no, or wait—not now. Doesn't
any loving parent give all three of these responses to a
child? Answering yes to every request would spoil you
and be dangerous to your well-being. Answering no
to every request would be vindictive, stingy, and de-
feating to your spirit. Answering wait to every prayer
would be frustrating. God always answers, but he does
so based on what he knows is best for you. When you
don't get the answer you want, don't misinterpret it as
silence from God but rather as a signal to point you in
a specific direction. Your spiritual maturity will grow
as you seek to understand how God's answer is what
is best for you.

DIVINE PROMISE

THE EYES OF THE LORD WATCH OVER THOSE
WHO DO RIGHT, AND HIS EARS ARE OPEN TO
THEIR PRAYERS. BUT THE LORD TURNS HIS
FACE AGAINST THOSE WHO DO EVIL.   *1 Peter 3:12*

Priorities

MY QUESTION *for* GOD

How do I set the right priorities?

A MOMENT *with* GOD

Seek [the Lord's] will in all you do, and he will show
you which path to take.   PROVERBS 3:6

As I looked at everything I had worked so hard to
accomplish, it was all so meaningless—like chasing
the wind. There was nothing really worthwhile
anywhere.   ECCLESIASTES 2:11

Martha was distracted by the big dinner she was
preparing. . . . But the Lord said to her, "My
dear Martha, you are worried and upset over all
these details! There is only one thing worth being
concerned about. Mary has discovered it, and it will
not be taken away from her."   LUKE 10:40-42

Wherever your treasure is, there the desires of your
heart will also be.   LUKE 12:34

*Y*ou're having a very personal and significant conversation with a friend at the kitchen table. Or you're
reading a Bible story with your young child just before tucking her in bed. Then the phone rings. Most
of us would answer the phone, or at least check the
caller ID, because interruptions tend to become top
priorities. Our lives often skip from one "urgent" inter-
ruption to another. And all the while we keep missing

what is really important. What things matter most in life? How can we distinguish true priorities from false ones, like the ringing phone? It's important that you don't confuse what's urgent with what's important. Therefore, you need to set your priorities first. Don't let everyone else decide what your day should look like—that should be between you and God. If you make time with him your first priority of the day, you will gain a God-given perspective on your activities for the rest of the day. As the famous theologian Martin Luther once said, "I am so busy now that if I did not spend two or three hours each day in prayer, I would not get through the day." Ask God to show you what is most important.

DIVINE PROMISE

SEEK THE KINGDOM OF GOD ABOVE ALL ELSE, AND LIVE RIGHTEOUSLY, AND HE WILL GIVE YOU EVERYTHING YOU NEED.   *Matthew 6:33*

Promises of God

MY QUESTION *for* GOD

How does knowing God help me believe his promises?

A MOMENT *with* GOD

O LORD God of Heaven's Armies! Where is there anyone as mighty as you, O LORD? You are entirely faithful.   PSALM 89:8

I bow before your holy Temple as I worship. I praise
your name for your unfailing love and faithfulness;
for your promises are backed by all the honor of
your name.   PSALM 138:2

*T*he trustworthiness of a promise depends on the answer to two questions: First, is the one making the
promise truthful and dependable? Second, does the
one making the promise have the ability to carry out
what he or he has promised? Both character and power
are crucial, and God possesses them in perfect degree.
If you can't believe a promise from God, you can't
believe a promise from anyone, because God alone is
completely trustworthy. You can be sure that God's
promises will come true, even when circumstances
might lead you to doubt. You can give your heart when
God gives his word.

DIVINE PROMISE
GOD CAN BE TRUSTED TO KEEP HIS PROMISE.
Hebrews 10:23

Purpose

MY QUESTION *for* GOD
How can I lead a more purposeful life?

A MOMENT *with* GOD

I cry out to God Most High, to God who will fulfill
his purpose for me.   PSALM 57:2

Your commandments give me understanding; no
wonder I hate every false way of life.   PSALM 119:104

Cry out for insight, and ask for understanding. Search
for them as you would for silver; seek them like
hidden treasures.   PROVERBS 2:3-4

My dear brothers and sisters, be strong and
immovable. Always work enthusiastically for the
Lord, for you know that nothing you do for the Lord
is ever useless.   1 CORINTHIANS 15:58

*U*nderstanding the deep truths that help life make sense
doesn't just happen; you have to search for understanding. You have to want to know why God made you and
what he wants you to do. If your best friend gave you a
letter before leaving on a trip and said, "Read this before
I get back," you would read it right away. God has left you
an entire book, the Bible, and has said, "Read this before
I return, because it tells you exactly what you need to
know to have a purposeful life." Will you read it?

DIVINE PROMISE

ALL SCRIPTURE IS INSPIRED BY GOD AND IS
USEFUL TO TEACH US WHAT IS TRUE. . . . GOD
USES IT TO PREPARE AND EQUIP HIS PEOPLE TO
DO EVERY GOOD WORK. *2 Timothy 3:16-17*

Purpose

I feel as if I'm supposed to do more in life. How can God help me discover what I was meant to do?

A Moment *with* God

I brought glory to you here on earth by completing the work you gave me to do.   JOHN 17:4

Everything comes from him and exists by his power and is intended for his glory.   ROMANS 11:36

Dear brothers and sisters, I plead with you to give your bodies to God because of all he has done for you. Let them be a living and holy sacrifice—the kind he will find acceptable. . . . Don't copy the behavior and customs of this world, but let God transform you into a new person by changing the way you think. Then you will learn to know God's will for you, which is good and pleasing and perfect.   ROMANS 12:1-2

We are busier than ever—in fact, many of us are downright frenzied. At the end of another frantic day, we slump in a chair or fall into bed and ask ourselves, "What did I do today? Did I make any difference?" Our lives often seem to lack a compelling purpose, a purpose worthy of our being created in God's image. And this aimlessness can lead to apathy and despair. But God has both a general purpose and a specific purpose for you. God has given you spiritual gifts and wants

you to use them to make a unique contribution in your
sphere of influence. The more you fulfill your general
purpose, the more clear your specific purpose will become. God calls you to partner with him in his great
redemptive plan for the world. Using your gifts to help
him fulfill that purpose will help you understand what
is truly important for you to accomplish each day and
to bring meaning to your work. It can fuel your energy
and ignite your dreams.

DIVINE PROMISE

I PRESS ON TO POSSESS THAT PERFECTION FOR
WHICH CHRIST JESUS FIRST POSSESSED ME.
Philippians 3:12

Pursuit by God

MY QUESTION *for* GOD

*The Bible says that God is pursuing me. Why would he
do that?*

A MOMENT *with* GOD

[God said,] "I thought to myself, 'I would love to
treat you as my own children!' I wanted nothing
more than to give you this beautiful land—the finest
possession in the world. I looked forward to your
calling me 'Father,' and I wanted you never to turn
from me."

JEREMIAH 3:19

I am writing to all of you in Rome who are loved by God and are called to be his own holy people.

ROMANS 1:7

See how very much our Father loves us, for he calls us his children, and that is what we are! But the people who belong to this world don't recognize that we are God's children because they don't know him.

1 JOHN 3:1

God is looking for a personal relationship with each person he has created. He pursues you not to get something from you but to give something wonderful to you: help, hope, power, salvation, joy, peace, and eternal life. He pursues you because he knows how much these gifts can transform your life forever. God's love relentlessly calls everyone to turn away from sin and to turn to an eternal relationship with him. While his desire is that no one reject him, he allows each person the freedom to return his love or to reject him and spend eternity apart from him. Will you be captivated by his pursuing, faithful love?

DIVINE PROMISE

LONG AGO THE LORD SAID TO ISRAEL:
"I HAVE LOVED YOU, MY PEOPLE, WITH AN
EVERLASTING LOVE. WITH UNFAILING LOVE
I HAVE DRAWN YOU TO MYSELF. *Jeremiah 31:3*

Quietness

MY QUESTION *for* GOD

Why are times of quietness important?

A MOMENT *with* GOD

Be still, and know that I am God! I will be honored
by every nation. I will be honored throughout
the world.   PSALM 46:10

*F*inding times to be quiet and meditate will help you
recognize the voice of God when he speaks.

Jesus said, "Let's go off by ourselves to a quiet place
and rest awhile." He said this because there were so
many people coming and going that Jesus and his
apostles didn't even have time to eat. So they left by
boat for a quiet place.   MARK 6:31-32

*J*esus saw the importance of spending time with
people, and likewise, the importance of rest and quiet
reflection. Life should have a balance of work and rest,
investment in people and quiet time for restoration.

It is crucial to renew your fellowship with God
and be restored by spending time with him. When you
connect with God, you tap into his strength. Maybe
you find it difficult to rest. You mistakenly believe that
productivity requires constant activity. But sometimes
you need to slow down in order to speed up; stop
awhile to let your body, mind, and spirit recover and

reset your purpose so that you can be more energized and productive when you are ready to get back to the work at hand.

"Go out and stand before me on the mountain," the LORD told [Elijah]. And as Elijah stood there, the LORD passed by, and a mighty windstorm hit the mountain. It was such a terrible blast that the rocks were torn loose, but the LORD was not in the wind. After the wind there was an earthquake, but the LORD was not in the earthquake. And after the earthquake there was a fire, but the LORD was not in the fire. And after the fire there was the sound of a gentle whisper. When Elijah heard it, he wrapped his face in his cloak and went out and stood at the entrance of the cave. And a voice said, "What are you doing here, Elijah?"   1 KINGS 19:11-13

Sometimes you must be still, quiet, and prepared in order to hear God speak. Sometimes you need to spend time with God without noise and distractions. Just meditate and listen for him to speak to your heart and mind.

When you pray, go away by yourself, shut the door behind you, and pray to your Father in private. Then your Father, who sees everything, will reward you.

                                            MATTHEW 6:6

*W*hen you need a quiet time of prayer, find a quiet place to escape from the busy world and allow God to speak to you.

Guard your heart above all else, for it determines the course of your life.   PROVERBS 4:23

*T*he best time to prepare for temptation is before it presses in on you. Train yourself in the quieter times so that you will have the spiritual wisdom, strength, and commitment to honor God in the face of intense temptation.

DIVINE CHALLENGE

THIS IS WHAT THE SOVEREIGN LORD,
THE HOLY ONE OF ISRAEL, SAYS: "ONLY IN
RETURNING TO ME AND RESTING IN ME
WILL YOU BE SAVED. IN QUIETNESS AND
CONFIDENCE IS YOUR STRENGTH." *Isaiah 30:15*

Quitting

MY QUESTION *for* GOD

How do I know when I need to keep going and when it's time to quit?

A MOMENT *with* GOD

David continued, "Be strong and courageous, and do the work. Don't be afraid or discouraged, for the LORD God, my God, is with you. He will not fail you or forsake you. He will see to it that all the work related to the Temple of the LORD is finished correctly.   1 CHRONICLES 28:20

Think carefully about what is right, and stop sinning.
                                        1 CORINTHIANS 15:34

We are pressed on every side by troubles, but we are not crushed. We are perplexed, but not driven to despair. . . . We know that God, who raised the Lord Jesus, will also raise us with Jesus and present us to himself together with you. . . . That is why we never give up.   2 CORINTHIANS 4:8, 14-16

It is time to quit when you are doing something wrong, when your actions are futile, or when you are hurting yourself or others. Even if your action or behavior is not inherently wrong, if it is not productive and is absorbing too much of your time and attention or is a stumbling block to others, it's time to quit. However, when God has called you to a task and you give up when it becomes difficult, you not only miss the great blessing of reaching your goal, but you might also incur discipline for not trusting God to help you get there. The fact that God asks you to do something doesn't make it easy. In fact, the harder the road, the stronger you become. If you know that God is in what you are doing or that he is taking you in a certain direction, don't give up just because the going gets tough. If anything, that should tell you that you are headed in the right direction. Keep moving forward with faith.

DIVINE ENCOURAGEMENT

LET'S NOT GET TIRED OF DOING WHAT IS GOOD. AT JUST THE RIGHT TIME WE WILL REAP A HARVEST OF BLESSING IF WE DON'T GIVE UP.
Galatians 6:9

Reconciliation

MY QUESTION *for* GOD

Why is being at peace with others important to God?

A MOMENT *with* GOD

If you are presenting a sacrifice at the altar in the Temple and you suddenly remember that someone has something against you, leave your sacrifice there at the altar. Go and be reconciled to that person. Then come and offer your sacrifice to God.   MATTHEW 5:23-24

God was in Christ, reconciling the world to himself, no longer counting people's sins against them. And he gave us this wonderful message of reconciliation.

2 CORINTHIANS 5:19

$\mathcal{R}$econciliation is the heart of what it means to follow Jesus. Jesus suffered the agony of the cross to redeem sinful human beings and reconcile them to a holy God. Your reconciliation with God is a picture of how you are to be reconciled with others. Harmony in human relationships is so important to Jesus that he commands you even to leave worship in order to first come clean with the people in your life with whom you have conflict. In other words, to live with an unresolved conflict actually hinders your relationship with God. Is there anyone in your life with whom Jesus wants you to pursue reconciliation?

DIVINE PROMISE

NOW WE CAN REJOICE IN OUR WONDERFUL NEW RELATIONSHIP WITH GOD BECAUSE OUR LORD JESUS CHRIST HAS MADE US FRIENDS OF GOD. *Romans 5:11*

Regrets

MY QUESTION *for* GOD

There are a lot of things in my past that I regret doing. How can I get over those regrets?

A Moment *with* God

[Jesus said,] "I say to you that you are Peter (which means 'rock'), and upon this rock I will build my church, and all the powers of hell will not conquer it."

MATTHEW 16:18

Peter was sitting outside in the courtyard. A servant girl came over and said to him, "You were one of those with Jesus the Galilean." But Peter denied it in front of everyone. "I don't know what you're talking about," he said. Later, out by the gate, another servant girl noticed him and said to those standing around, "This man was with Jesus of Nazareth." Again Peter denied it, this time with an oath. "I don't even know the man," he said. A little later some of the other bystanders came over to Peter and said, "You must be one of them; we can tell by your Galilean accent." Peter swore, "A curse on me if I'm lying—I don't know the man!" And immediately the rooster crowed. Suddenly, Jesus' words flashed through Peter's mind: "Before the rooster crows, you will deny three times that you even know me." And he went away, weeping bitterly. MATTHEW 26:69-75

Anyone who belongs to Christ has become a new person. The old life is gone; a new life has begun!

2 CORINTHIANS 5:17

If the memories and experiences of our lives were rocks, collected and carried in a backpack, surely guilt and regret would be among the heaviest. A sense of guilt is the legitimate spiritual response to sin; regret is the sorrow over the consequences of your decisions, both those that are sinful and those that are simply unfortunate. God promises to remove the guilt of all who seek his forgiveness, but he does not prevent the consequences of your sin. It is the weight of regret over those consequences that weighs you down. God promises to help you deal with your regrets so that you can move on without carrying a load of guilt. When you come to faith in Jesus, he forgives your sins—all of them. He chooses not to remember your past, and he gives you a fresh start. You will still have to live with the consequences of your sins, because they cannot be retracted. But because God forgives you, you can move forward without the tremendous guilt that can accompany regret. Because God no longer holds your sins against you, you can be free from self-condemnation. Regrets can be so enslaving that they consume your thoughts and keep you from serving God. If Peter had continued to focus on his regret over denying Jesus, he would never have been able to preach the Good News so powerfully. Don't let regret paralyze you; instead, let God's forgiveness motivate you to positive action for him in the future. It is a divine moment when you truly grasp the power of God's forgiveness, because then you are able to turn your regrets into resolve.

Divine Promise

DAVID ALSO SPOKE OF THIS WHEN HE
DESCRIBED THE HAPPINESS OF THOSE WHO
ARE DECLARED RIGHTEOUS WITHOUT

WORKING FOR IT: "OH, WHAT JOY FOR THOSE
WHOSE DISOBEDIENCE IS FORGIVEN, WHOSE
SINS ARE PUT OUT OF SIGHT. YES, WHAT JOY
FOR THOSE WHOSE RECORD THE LORD HAS
CLEARED OF SIN." *Romans 4:6-8*

Relationship

MY QUESTION *for* GOD

How does God pursue a relationship with me?

A MOMENT *with* GOD

When the cool evening breezes were blowing, the
man and his wife heard the LORD God walking about
in the garden. So they hid from the LORD God among
the trees. Then the LORD God called to the man,
"Where are you?"   GENESIS 3:8-9

Surely your goodness and unfailing love will pursue
me all the days of my life.   PSALM 23:6

[Jesus said,] "I will ask the Father, and he will give
you another Advocate, who will never leave you. He
is the Holy Spirit, who leads into all truth."

JOHN 14:16-17

Adam and Eve sinned in disobeying God and rebel-
ling against him. And yet the first thing God did was
pursue them in order to restore their relationship with
him. Although Adam and Eve would have to experi-

ence the consequences of their actions, God had no intention of severing the relationship. It's hard to imagine this kind of complete unconditional love that pursues you no matter what you have done. When you do what is wrong, or when you reject God, he does not give up on you but rather pursues you for the purpose of forgiving your sin and restoring you to a right relationship with him. God pursues you by causing regret or guilt in your heart—Jesus taught that one of the roles of the Holy Spirit is to convince you when you have sinned. God also pursues you by the truth of his Word, which calls you to confession and repentance. God's faithful pursuit is a beautiful call to friendship with him. Will you respond?

DIVINE PROMISE

LONG AGO THE LORD SAID TO ISRAEL:
"I HAVE LOVED YOU, MY PEOPLE, WITH AN
EVERLASTING LOVE. WITH UNFAILING LOVE
I HAVE DRAWN YOU TO MYSELF." *Jeremiah 31:3*

Renewal

MY QUESTION *for* GOD

My life is a mess, and I feel as if I need to start over again. How can I experience renewal?

A MOMENT *with* GOD

Create in me a clean heart, O God. Renew a loyal
spirit within me.   PSALM 51:10

"Come now, let's settle this," says the LORD. "Though
your sins are like scarlet, I will make them as white as
snow. Though they are red like crimson, I will make
them as white as wool."   ISAIAH 1:18

I will give you a new heart, and I will put a new spirit
in you. I will take out your stony, stubborn heart and
give you a tender, responsive heart.   EZEKIEL 36:26

Throw off your old sinful nature and your former
way of life, which is corrupted by lust and deception.
Instead, let the Spirit renew your thoughts and
attitudes. Put on your new nature, created to be like
God—truly righteous and holy.   EPHESIANS 4:21-24

How often we disappoint ourselves. We have such
high hopes and good intentions but inevitably, we find
ourselves weary and burnt out with self-defeat, the
burdens of everyday living, or the consequences of bad
choices and sinful actions. The messiness of life can
leave us feeling exhausted not only physically but in our
very souls as well. If only we could start over.

Renewal begins with the compassion of God and
a heart ready for change. When the two are put together, you find a new beginning, a soul refreshed,
and a life revived. God makes it clear he will restore
any heart that seeks a new start. That new start begins
with a sincere desire to turn to God and turn away

from what has been bringing you down. To begin, ask God to forgive your sin, which poisons everything you do. Thank God that his forgiveness is not based on the magnitude of your sin but on the magnitude of his love. Only one sin is too great for God's unconditional love and forgiveness: an attitude of defiant, hostile rejection of God, which prevents you from accepting his forgiveness. Those who don't want his forgiveness are beyond its reach. But a heart that truly wants to change is a heart that is ready for the renewal that only God's Spirit can bring.

DIVINE PROMISE
ANYONE WHO BELONGS TO CHRIST HAS BECOME A NEW PERSON. THE OLD LIFE IS GONE; A NEW LIFE HAS BEGUN! *2 Corinthians 5:17*

Respect

MY QUESTIONS *for* GOD
Where can I find a little respect these days? What does God say about getting respect?

A MOMENT *with* GOD
I pressed further, "What you are doing is not right!"
NEHEMIAH 5:9

Whoever wants to be a leader among you must be your servant.
MATTHEW 20:26

[Jesus] must become greater and greater, and I must
become less and less.   JOHN 3:30

The keys to respect may not be what you expect.
Respect comes from serving rather than from being
served. Respect comes from taking responsibility for
your actions instead of trying to save face in front of
others. Respect comes from speaking up when things
are wrong instead of blending in with the group. Respect comes from building others up instead of trying
to make yourself look good.

The world teaches you to look beautiful at all
costs and to act confidently even when you're scared,
to speak with irreverence, and to live by what's best for
you. In the end, these self-centered practices will bring
only dishonor in the eyes of your peers. True respect is
reserved for people who consistently practice kindness,
live with integrity, and are motivated by a deep love for
others. The more you reflect the character of God, the
more you will become the kind of woman who truly
earns respect.

DIVINE PROMISE

THERE WILL BE GLORY AND HONOR AND PEACE
FROM GOD FOR ALL WHO DO GOOD.   *Romans 2:10*

Responsibility

MY QUESTION *for* GOD

Am I really responsible for my actions? I can't help it when I do certain things.

A MOMENT *with* GOD

Do not let sin control the way you live; do not give in to sinful desires. Do not let any part of your body become an instrument of evil to serve sin. Instead, give yourselves completely to God, for you were dead, but now you have new life. So use your whole body as an instrument to do what is right for the glory of God. Sin is no longer your master, for you no longer live under the requirements of the law. Instead, you live under the freedom of God's grace.

ROMANS 6:12-14

The term *bad habit* brings to mind activities such as smoking, overeating, and alcohol or drug abuse. But spreading gossip, complaining, chronic worrying, and backbiting are bad habits too. One of Satan's great lies is that you are a victim who has no power to resist your impulses. The world teaches that heredity, environment, and circumstances excuse you from responsibility. In reality, everything you do is the result of a choice you make, and you are responsible for those choices. Yes, it's hard to resist certain temptations and always make good choices. But you have no one but yourself to blame for your bad choices.

The good news is that God is more powerful than anything that seeks to control you. When you tap into his power through prayer and ask for the support of fellow believers, God breaks the chains that hold you and you develop the strength to say no.

DIVINE PROMISE

DON'T YOU REALIZE THAT YOU BECOME THE
SLAVE OF WHATEVER YOU CHOOSE TO OBEY?
YOU CAN BE A SLAVE TO SIN, WHICH LEADS TO
DEATH, OR YOU CAN CHOOSE TO OBEY GOD,
WHICH LEADS TO RIGHTEOUS LIVING.

Romans 6:16

Rest

MY QUESTION *for* GOD

Why is rest so important for me?

A MOMENT *with* GOD

The creation of the heavens and the earth and everything in them was completed. On the seventh day God had finished his work of creation, so he rested from all his work. And God blessed the seventh day and declared it holy, because it was the day when he rested from all his work of creation.

GENESIS 2:1-3

[God said,] "It is a permanent sign of my covenant with the people of Israel. For in six days the LORD

made heaven and earth, but on the seventh day he
stopped working and was refreshed."   Exodus 31:17

The Lord is my shepherd; I have all that I need. He
lets me rest in green meadows; he leads me beside
peaceful streams. He renews my strength. He guides
me along right paths, bringing honor to his name.

Psalm 23:1-3

It is useless for you to work so hard from early
morning until late at night, anxiously working for
food to eat; for God gives rest to his loved ones.

Psalm 127:2

Ours is an age of anxiety and stress because it is an
age of perpetual motion. We take pride in explaining
to each other how busy we are, and we feel guilty if we
relax. God did not intend for his people to live in a state
of frenzied activity. From his own example in Genesis
to the promises of the New Testament, it is clear that
God wants us to take time for rest and refreshment
for our bodies and our souls. Why would the omnip-
otent God of the universe rest following his work of
creation? Surely, it wasn't because the Almighty was
physically tired! The answer is that God, in ceasing
from his work, called his rest "holy." God knew that
you would need to cease from your work to care for
your physical and spiritual needs. Work is good, but it
must be balanced by regular rest and attention to the
health of your soul. Otherwise, you miss the divine

moments God sends your way. Make sure to carve out regular times for worship and spiritual refreshment.

DIVINE PROMISE

JESUS SAID, "COME TO ME, ALL OF YOU WHO ARE WEARY AND CARRY HEAVY BURDENS, AND I WILL GIVE YOU REST."   *Matthew 11:28*

Risk

MY QUESTION *for* GOD

What happens when I take risks for God?

A MOMENT *with* GOD

Esther told Hathach to go back and relay this message to Mordecai: "All the king's officials and even the people in the provinces know that anyone who appears before the king in his inner court without being invited is doomed to die unless the king holds out his gold scepter. And the king has not called for me to come to him for thirty days." So Hathach gave Esther's message to Mordecai. Mordecai sent this reply to Esther: "Don't think for a moment that because you're in the palace you will escape when all other Jews are killed. If you keep quiet at a time like this, deliverance and relief for the Jews will arise from some other place, but you and your relatives will die. Who knows if perhaps you were made queen for just such a time as this?"   ESTHER 4:10-14

*M*ost of us try to minimize risk. We have insurance policies, individual retirement funds, security codes on credit cards, and alarm systems in our homes and cars. The need to protect yourself is not a bad thing unless it keeps you from doing what you want to do, have to do, or are called by God to do. The Bible warns that the Christian life can be risky but worth it if your goals are spiritual growth and success in God's eyes. Taking a risk entails having a good goal, a decent chance of achieving it, and a strong dose of confidence. Queen Esther, through her consistent character, had won the trust of the king and thus had increased her chances of being successful. Taking risks is actually necessary if you want to grow in your relationship with God. When he calls you to do something outside your comfort zone, obey at the risk of failing, while trusting him to help you complete what he has asked you to do. Then your growth will take giant steps.

DIVINE PROMISE

COMMIT EVERYTHING YOU DO TO THE LORD. TRUST HIM, AND HE WILL HELP YOU. *Psalm 37:5*

Romance

MY QUESTION *for* GOD

How can I keep romance alive in my marriage?

A Moment *with* God

Come, my love, let us go out to the fields and spend the night among the wildflowers. Let us get up early and go to the vineyards to see if the grapevines have budded, if the blossoms have opened, and if the pomegranates have bloomed. There I will give you my love.   SONG OF SONGS 7:11-12

Place me like a seal over your heart. . . . For love is as strong as death.   SONG OF SONGS 8:6

Spontaneity and variety are key ingredients of romance. Dull routine destroys romance. So surprise your husband by doing something unexpected and spontaneous. Take a weekend just for the two of you. Send flowers. Stick a love note on the bathroom mirror. Call him just to tell him you love him. When you were dating, you probably did those things. Start doing them again, and watch romance bloom again.

Song of Songs is a book about the romantic love of husbands and wives. True, romantic, marital love is exclusive and permanent, sealing your heart in faithfulness to your mate. Romantic feelings come through giving love, not by focusing on receiving love. Love is an offering of yourself rather than a claim of how someone else should treat you. Just as God pursues you with his unconditional love, romance is the art of pursuing your mate with that same unconditional love.

DIVINE PROMISE

I AM GIVING YOU A NEW COMMANDMENT:
LOVE EACH OTHER. JUST AS I HAVE LOVED YOU,
YOU SHOULD LOVE EACH OTHER.   *John 13:34*

Romance

MY QUESTION *for* GOD

Where's the romance in a life of faith?

A MOMENT *with* GOD

Long ago the LORD said to Israel: "I have loved you,
my people, with an everlasting love. With unfailing
love I have drawn you to myself."   JEREMIAH 31:3

[The Lord said,] "I will win her back once again. I
will lead her into the desert and speak tenderly to her
there. . . . I will make you my wife forever, showing
you righteousness and justice, unfailing love and
compassion. I will be faithful to you and make you
mine, and you will finally know me as the LORD."

HOSEA 2:14, 19-20

Let us be glad and rejoice, and let us give honor to
him. For the time has come for the wedding feast of
the Lamb, and his bride has prepared herself.

REVELATION 19:7

*R*omance is the language of love that fosters intimacy with another person. What a wonderful feeling when someone expresses his or her affection for you, enjoys your company, and is captivated by you. You feel confident, strong, and interesting to that person. As you read through the Bible, you learn that God himself is a romantic who desires an intimate relationship with you. He desires your constant company and is interested in the smallest details of your life. He wants nothing more than to walk with you through this life and for all eternity. As you realize your precious value to God, you will find confidence in your faith, strength to be faithful to him, and a deep hunger and desire to know more of him.

DIVINE PROMISE

SURELY YOUR GOODNESS AND UNFAILING
LOVE WILL PURSUE ME ALL THE DAYS OF
MY LIFE.   *Psalm 23:6*

Sacrifice

MY QUESTION *for* GOD

Why is it good to make a habit of sacrificing for others?

A MOMENT *with* GOD

Lay your hand on the animal's head, and the LORD will accept its death in your place to purify you, making you right with him.   LEVITICUS 1:4

The law of Moses was unable to save us because of the weakness of our sinful nature. So God did what the law could not do. He sent his own Son in a body like the bodies we sinners have. And in that body God declared an end to sin's control over us by giving his Son as a sacrifice for our sins.   ROMANS 8:3

This is real love—not that we loved God, but that he loved us and sent his Son as a sacrifice to take away our sins.   1 JOHN 4:10

𝒜 sacrifice is a giving up of one thing in order to obtain something of greater value. Parents may sacrifice a new car to save money for a child's education. A baseball player executes a "sacrifice bunt" to give a teammate an opportunity to score a run. In the Old Testament, a sacrifice was an act of worship in which the blood of an animal was shed as a substitute for the punishment a person's sin deserved. It seems strange and even barbaric that animals would be sacrificed on an altar almost continually. But how much worse if a person had to die instead?

Today we are desensitized to the seriousness of sin. But sin is just as serious to God as it has always been. Sin deserves eternal death because it separates us from God. God is holy; we are not. Holiness and sin cannot coexist. In Old Testament days, God provided a way for the people's sins to be removed so they could be holy in God's eyes. The animals people brought to the altar to be sacrificed would become their "substitutes." The people symbolically transferred their sins to the animal before it was sacrificed, allowing them to be pure and holy once again, but it was only temporary. When Jesus died on the cross, he transferred our sins onto himself forever (read Hebrews 9:11-15; 10:11-18). Because Jesus' sacrifice was perfect, no more sacrifices are necessary. All you must do now is recognize your sin before God and accept his gift of forgiveness. Anytime you make a sacrifice by giving something up for someone else, you are reminded, in some small way, of God's greatest sacrifice of all.

DIVINE PROMISE

JUST AS EACH PERSON IS DESTINED TO DIE ONCE AND AFTER THAT COMES JUDGMENT, SO ALSO CHRIST DIED ONCE FOR ALL TIME AS A SACRIFICE TO TAKE AWAY THE SINS OF MANY PEOPLE. HE WILL COME AGAIN, NOT TO DEAL WITH OUR SINS, BUT TO BRING SALVATION TO ALL WHO ARE EAGERLY WAITING FOR HIM.

Hebrews 9:27-28

Security

MY QUESTION *for* GOD

How does knowing God give me true security?

A MOMENT *with* GOD

God's way is perfect. All the LORD's promises prove true.   PSALM 18:30

Those who trust in the LORD are as secure as Mount
Zion; they will not be defeated but will endure
forever.   PSALM 125:1

The grass withers and the flowers fade, but the word
of our God stands forever.   ISAIAH 40:8

If you confess with your mouth that Jesus is Lord and
believe in your heart that God raised him from the
dead, you will be saved.   ROMANS 10:9

From retirement investment portfolios to home-
protection systems, we spend vast amounts of time
and money on security. Financial security, personal
security, job security, relational security, and even na-
tional security are sooner or later threatened by the
unpredictable nature of the world in which we live.
Despite the changing nature of the world around you,
you can always be truly secure about two things: First,
when you make decisions and live each day based on the
changeless truths of God's Word, you have complete
assurance that you are doing the right thing. There are
fundamental principles of right and wrong, true and
false, good and bad that never change because God
established them at the creation of the universe. Follow these biblical principles, and you can be secure in
knowing that what you are doing is not only right but
also pleasing to God. When you build your faith day
by day on the truths of God's Word, you have built a
solid foundation that will not easily crack under the
world's pressure.

Second, you can be certain that your eternal future is secure in heaven when you believe that Jesus Christ is the Son of God who died to forgive your sins and rose again to live forever. When Jesus rose from the dead, he proved that he has power over death and therefore gives you the confidence that his promise that you will live forever is certain.

DIVINE PROMISE

GOD LOVED THE WORLD SO MUCH THAT HE GAVE HIS ONE AND ONLY SON, SO THAT EVERYONE WHO BELIEVES IN HIM WILL NOT PERISH BUT HAVE ETERNAL LIFE. *John 3:16*

Self-Esteem

MY QUESTION *for* GOD

How can I overcome my insecurities to become a secure, confident woman?

A MOMENT *with* GOD

Not a single sparrow can fall to the ground without your Father knowing it. . . . You are more valuable to God than a whole flock of sparrows.   MATTHEW 10:29-31

Be honest in your evaluation of yourselves, measuring yourselves by the faith God has given us.   ROMANS 12:3

We are God's masterpiece. He has created us anew in Christ Jesus, so we can do the good things he planned for us long ago.   EPHESIANS 2:10

You should clothe yourselves instead with the beauty that comes from within, the unfading beauty of a gentle and quiet spirit, which is so precious to God.

1 PETER 3:4

To think more highly of yourself than you should is pride. But to think less of yourself than you should is false humility. In one sense that can be pride too: pride in your supposed humility. In between, there is an honest appraisal of your own worth based on who you are in God, and that is self-esteem. God values you highly because he loves you deeply. But you must not think you are sufficient without God. Your sufficiency is in God. Your value is tied to the value he places on you and the purpose for which he created you. That makes you a woman of great value indeed.

If you struggle with insecurity, it may mean that you're measuring your value by the wrong things. The only thing that matters—and the only way to be secure—is to find your value as a creation of God, one of his masterpieces. Because of God's power within you, you should have a healthy and confident self-esteem, because with him you are capable of doing far more than you could ever dare to dream.

DIVINE PROMISE

HOW PRECIOUS ARE YOUR THOUGHTS ABOUT ME, O GOD.   *Psalm 139:17*

Sensitivity

MY QUESTION *for* GOD

How can I become more sensitive to others' needs?

A MOMENT *with* GOD

If your gift is to encourage others, be encouraging. If it is giving, give generously. If God has given you leadership ability, take the responsibility seriously. And if you have a gift for showing kindness to others, do it gladly.   ROMANS 12:8

When God's people are in need, be ready to help them. Always be eager to practice hospitality.

ROMANS 12:13

You must all be quick to listen, slow to speak, and slow to get angry.   JAMES 1:19

All of you should be of one mind. Sympathize with each other. Love each other as brothers and sisters. Be tenderhearted, and keep a humble attitude.

1 PETER 3:8

*W*ho wants to be around a person who couldn't care less about others? Who enjoys being around an overly sensitive person who always seems to get hurt by whatever is said? Sensitivity in proper balance, however, is a beautiful quality. Most people are attracted to sensitive people because they care deeply about others without smothering or manipulating them or becoming jealous or controlling. Ironically, both insensitivity and oversensitivity are products of a self-centered focus, and both can be changed by focusing on others rather than on yourself.

Sensitivity reflects alertness to others and responds appropriately to their feelings. You can become more sensitive by listening to others, considering how their situation is affected by their feelings and struggles, showing respect for others and their perspectives, and being willing to lay aside your own needs to treat others with gentleness and care. God has equipped you in special ways to meet the needs of others around you. When you put aside your own agenda, listen carefully, and act thoughtfully, you are developing the kind of sensitive heart that is so precious to God and that touches others right where they need it most.

DIVINE PROMISE

DON'T FORGET TO DO GOOD AND TO SHARE WITH THOSE IN NEED. THESE ARE THE SACRIFICES THAT PLEASE GOD. *Hebrews 13:16*

Sensitivity

MY QUESTION *for* GOD

What will dull my spiritual sensitivity?

A MOMENT *with* GOD

I said, "It's all over! I am doomed, for I am a sinful man. I have filthy lips, and I live among a people with filthy lips. Yet I have seen the King, the LORD of Heaven's Armies."   ISAIAH 6:5

A lack of a fresh awareness of God's holiness will dull your sensitivity to the sin in your life.

The prophecy of Isaiah . . . says, "When you hear what I say, you will not understand. When you see what I do, you will not comprehend. For the hearts of these people are hardened, and their ears cannot hear, and they have closed their eyes." MATTHEW 13:14-15

Giving up on fighting evil and giving in to sinful desires will dull your spiritual sensitivity.

Anyone who wanders away from this teaching has no relationship with God.   2 JOHN 1:9

Time away from God's truth dulls your spiritual sensitivities. The more you ignore God, the less sensitive you will be toward his presence and his leading.

[God said,] "I have a few complaints against you.
You tolerate some among you whose teaching is like
that of Balaam, who showed Balak how to trip up
the people of Israel. He taught them to sin . . . by
committing sexual sin.   REVELATION 2:14

*C*ompromising with sin will eventually dull your sensitivity to it.

Open my eyes to see the wonderful truths in your
instructions.   PSALM 119:18

Jesus told him, "I entered this world to render
judgment—to give sight to the blind and to show
those who think they see that they are blind."

                                           JOHN 9:39

They stumble because they do not obey God's word.

                                           1 PETER 2:8

*S*piritual sensitivity comes from eyes that are open
to God's Word and ears that are willing to hear it.
Develop the art of listening to God through his Word.
Then put your hands into action!

DIVINE PROMISE
I WILL GIVE THEM SINGLENESS OF HEART AND
PUT A NEW SPIRIT WITHIN THEM. I WILL TAKE
AWAY THEIR STONY, STUBBORN HEART AND
GIVE THEM A TENDER, RESPONSIVE HEART.
Ezekiel 11:19

Service

What are the right attitudes to have for effective service
to God?

A MOMENT *with* GOD

Serve the LORD with reverent fear, and rejoice with
trembling.   PSALM 2:11

A joyful heart and reverent awe of God are required
in order to serve him. Being a servant of God is not a
dull obligation but a great privilege. Service should be
done joyfully and with gratitude for the opportunity
and ability to serve.

I will search for faithful people to be my companions.
Only those who are above reproach will be allowed
to serve me.   PSALM 101:6

A desire to please God and obey his Word are essential in order to serve him effectively. A good quality at work is a desire to please your boss and to act
in accordance with company rules and fulfill your job
description. Neglecting these responsibilities would
lead to termination. A desire to please God and obey
his commandments qualifies you for lifelong effective
service for him.

No one can serve two masters. For you will hate one and love the other; you will be devoted to one and despise the other. You cannot serve both God and money.

MATTHEW 6:24

*I*n order to serve God effectively, you must be devoted to him. This involves sacrifice, and effective service comes at a cost. You must be willing to sacrifice some of your own comforts and desires in order to effectively reach out to those who need God most.

You have been called to live in freedom, my brothers and sisters. But don't use your freedom to satisfy your sinful nature. Instead, use your freedom to serve one another in love.

GALATIANS 5:13

*E*ffective service requires a heart filled with genuine love for Christ and others. Serving God inevitably means serving others. If your heart is always focused on your own desires first, you will not be as effective at helping others. Genuine love means genuine selflessness and the self-discipline to put others first.

DIVINE PROMISE

EVEN THE SON OF MAN CAME NOT TO BE
SERVED BUT TO SERVE OTHERS AND TO GIVE
HIS LIFE AS A RANSOM FOR MANY. *Mark 10:45*

Sharing

How can I be motivated to share more?

A MOMENT *with* GOD

There's a young boy here with five barley loaves and
two fish. But what good is that with this huge crowd?

JOHN 6:9

I always thank my God for you and for the gracious
gifts he has given you, now that you belong to
Christ Jesus.   1 CORINTHIANS 1:4

As each part does its own special work, it helps the
other parts grow, so that the whole body is healthy
and growing and full of love.   EPHESIANS 4:16

Almost everyone has been taught since early child-
hood to share. Yet for many people it remains as hard
as ever to give of their resources or themselves. Why?
Because at the very core of sinful human nature is the
desire to get, not give; to accumulate, not relinquish;
to look out for yourself, not others. The Bible calls
you to share many things—your resources, your faith,
your love, your time, your talents, your money. In fact,
most things are more enjoyable when you share them
with others, and doing so benefits others far more than
you may realize. The boy in John 6 shared his lunch
with Jesus, who multiplied it to feed a hungry multi-

tude. Five thousand people were blessed by this one selfless act.

Like this boy, you are called to share because God shares so generously with you. Sharing is an expression of your love for God, demonstrated in your love for others. As you share your special gifts and resources, you pass on God's blessings. Those who generously share discover that the benefits of giving away are far greater than the temporary satisfaction of receiving.

DIVINE PROMISE

MAY YOU BE FILLED WITH JOY, ALWAYS THANKING THE FATHER. HE HAS ENABLED YOU TO SHARE IN THE INHERITANCE THAT BELONGS TO HIS PEOPLE, WHO LIVE IN THE LIGHT. *Colossians 1:11-12*

Significance

MY QUESTION *for* GOD

My life feels so small and insignificant. How can I make it count for God?

A MOMENT *with* GOD

Do not despise these small beginnings, for the LORD rejoices to see the work begin.　　　　　ZECHARIAH 4:10

My life is worth nothing to me unless I use it for finishing the work assigned me by the Lord Jesus—

the work of telling others the Good News about the
wonderful grace of God.   ACTS 20:24

*D*eep within every human heart is a yearning for
our lives to count, to make a difference, to be worth
something. Most people struggle with feeling insignificant—that they're not doing anything truly important
or making a difference. And many people spend far
more time being paralyzed by what they cannot do than
acting on what they can do; their inabilities overshadow
their abilities. Everywhere they look they see others
who are more successful, more gifted, more this, more
that. It is no wonder so many of us feel insignificant!

But one of the great lessons of the Bible is that
the heroes of the faith—people like Moses, Gideon,
Esther, and Peter—were ordinary people who learned
that their significance came not from what *they* could
accomplish with their abilities, but from what *God*
could accomplish through their abilities. Significance
comes first from knowing that you have been created
by God, who has given you specific abilities he wants
to use for his purpose. When you use your God-given
abilities to accomplish his work, your life becomes significant both now and for eternity.

DIVINE PROMISE

REMEMBER, DEAR BROTHERS AND SISTERS,
THAT FEW OF YOU WERE WISE IN THE WORLD'S
EYES OR POWERFUL OR WEALTHY WHEN GOD
CALLED YOU. *1 Corinthians 1:26*

Simplicity

MY QUESTION for GOD

How can I simplify my life?

A MOMENT with GOD

Jesus said, "That is why I tell you not to worry about everyday life—whether you have enough food to eat or enough clothes to wear. For life is more than food, and your body more than clothing." LUKE 12:22-23

Live in harmony with each other. Don't be too proud to enjoy the company of ordinary people. And don't think you know it all! ROMANS 12:16

Simplicity is not just a lifestyle but a tangible expression of an inner attitude of the heart. There are three main components to an attitude of simplicity: (1) thankfulness—viewing every possession and good occurrence as a gift from God; (2) trust—that your life and everything about it is ultimately under the care of God, not you; and (3) generosity—being willing to share all you have with others. When you are thankful, you expect nothing but are delighted with everything. When you trust that everything belongs to God and is in his care, you free yourself from worry and anxiety. Finally, when you share as an expression of God's own generosity toward you, you hold things loosely. When these three attitudes work together, you are freed from the slavery of materialism and can live a life of simplicity.

DIVINE PROMISE

THIS WORLD IS FADING AWAY, ALONG WITH
EVERYTHING THAT PEOPLE CRAVE. BUT
ANYONE WHO DOES WHAT PLEASES GOD WILL
LIVE FOREVER.   *1 John 2:17*

Sorrow

MY QUESTION *for* GOD

Will joy ever overcome the sorrows of life?

A MOMENT *with* GOD

Weeping may last through the night, but joy comes
with the morning.   PSALM 30:5

What joy for those whose strength comes from the
LORD, who have set their minds on a pilgrimage to
Jerusalem. When they walk through the Valley of
Weeping, it will become a place of refreshing springs.
The autumn rains will clothe it with blessings. They
will continue to grow stronger, and each of them will
appear before God in Jerusalem.   PSALM 84:5-7

While the Bible does not identify a specific valley as
the Valley of Weeping, it is thought that the pilgrimage
to the Temple in Jerusalem passed through a barren
valley of that name. The word *weeping* may have been a
symbolic reference to times of struggle and tears that
are often part of life—even for people on their way
to meet with God. Whether predictable or random,

the tragic losses of life affect all of us profoundly. The Bible acknowledges that sorrow and grief are part of human life. The psalm writer is clearly showing that faith in God does not keep you from going through difficult times; rather, it enables you to walk through those times and grow stronger along the way. You can take heart because sorrow does not have the last word. God redeems your losses with his promises of comfort and hope.

When you walk through your own Valley of Weeping, keep walking toward God. Don't take a path away from him. God promises to relieve your sorrow and one day replace it with joy that lasts forever.

DIVINE PROMISE

HE WILL WIPE EVERY TEAR FROM THEIR EYES, AND THERE WILL BE NO MORE DEATH OR SORROW OR CRYING OR PAIN.   *Revelation 21:4*

Spiritual Gifts

MY QUESTION *for* GOD

How can I make myself more available for God's use?

A MOMENT *with* GOD

I heard the Lord asking, "Whom should I send as a messenger to this people? Who will go for us?" I said, "Here I am. Send me."   ISAIAH 6:8

A spiritual gift is given to each of us so we can help each other. To one person the Spirit gives the ability to give wise advice; to another the same Spirit gives a message of special knowledge. The same Spirit gives great faith to another, and to someone else the one Spirit gives the gift of healing. . . . In fact, some parts of the body that seem weakest and least important are actually the most necessary.   1 CORINTHIANS 12:7-9, 22

God has given each of you a gift from his great variety of spiritual gifts. Use them well to serve one another.

1 PETER 4:10

Being available to God includes the continual development of the gifts he has given you so that you will be prepared for him to use you. It involves your willingness to use those gifts to serve him in the calling he currently has for you. Do you know the unique gifts God has given you? If not, you might consider taking a spiritual-gifts assessment and ask your friends what they think your gifts are. It is important to know that God gives each individual a spiritual gift—sometimes more than one!—and a special ministry in the church where you can use those gifts to help and encourage others and to bring glory to his name. When you use these spiritual gifts, you help fulfill the purpose for which God made you. You can never use up these spiritual gifts; rather, the more you use them, the more they grow and allow you to make a unique contribution in your sphere of influence. It is a divine moment when you find the place where you can be most effective for

God and when you do your best work for God in helping others.

DIVINE PROMISE

THIS IS WHY I REMIND YOU TO FAN INTO
FLAMES THE SPIRITUAL GIFT GOD GAVE
YOU WHEN I LAID MY HANDS ON YOU. FOR
GOD HAS NOT GIVEN US A SPIRIT OF FEAR
AND TIMIDITY, BUT OF POWER, LOVE, AND
SELF-DISCIPLINE.   *2 Timothy 1:6-7*

Spiritual Growth

MY QUESTION *for* GOD

What is the beauty of steady spiritual progress?

A MOMENT *with* GOD

Commit everything you do to the LORD. Trust him,
and he will help you. He will make your innocence
radiate like the dawn, and the justice of your cause
will shine like the noonday sun.   PSALM 37:5-6

The way of the righteous is like the first gleam of
dawn, which shines ever brighter until the full light
of day.   PROVERBS 4:18

*T*here are few things more glorious than a beautiful
sunrise. As that yellow ball rises above the horizon,
it promises a new day with new beginnings and new

opportunities. Its light and warmth bring growth and strength to all living things. The Bible compares your relationship with the Lord to the rising sun. Your love relationship with God is the source of your daily strength in every situation. His love and care for you warm your soul and give you hope. The Author of life is also the Author of strength and hope. As you commit your life to him, you reflect his brilliant glory more and more.

DIVINE PROMISE

THE LORD—WHO IS THE SPIRIT—MAKES
US MORE AND MORE LIKE HIM AS WE ARE
CHANGED INTO HIS GLORIOUS IMAGE.
2 Corinthians 3:18

Spiritual Warfare

MY QUESTION *for* GOD

Are there really spiritual enemies—powers of darkness—trying to get me?

A MOMENT *with* GOD

Then he said, "Don't be afraid, Daniel. Since the first day you began to pray for understanding and to humble yourself before your God, your request has been heard in heaven. I have come in answer to your prayer. But for twenty-one days the spirit prince of the kingdom of Persia blocked my way.

Then Michael, one of the archangels, came to help me, and I left him there with the spirit prince of the kingdom of Persia."
                                        DANIEL 10:12-13

Jesus was led by the Spirit into the wilderness to be tempted there by the devil.   MATTHEW 4:1

𝒯he Bible clearly teaches that human beings are involved in a spiritual battle. Far from excluding you from this spiritual battle, faith puts you right in the middle of it. You are in a battle for your very soul. You must recognize that and arm yourself, or you will be overwhelmed.

The enemy who planted the weeds among the wheat is the devil.   MATTHEW 13:39

We are not fighting against flesh-and-blood enemies, but against evil rulers and authorities of the unseen world, against mighty powers in this dark world, and against evil spirits in the heavenly places. EPHESIANS 6:12

𝒮atan is alive and active, and his legions of demons are always on the attack. A battle rages in the spiritual realm—a battle you can't see but one you will experience if you seek to serve God. You need God's power, not your own, to stand strong and not allow temptation to overcome you. Most of all, since you do not always know or understand the evil that is threatening you, you need God's power to give you strength to face an unknown enemy. Have peace that God has already won the battle over death and has the power to save you.

DIVINE PROMISE

THE LORD IS FAITHFUL; HE WILL STRENGTHEN YOU AND GUARD YOU FROM THE EVIL ONE.
2 Thessalonians 3:3

Strengths and Weaknesses

MY QUESTION *for* GOD

What happens when I learn to use my strengths and weaknesses for God?

A MOMENT *with* GOD

Don't be afraid, for I am with you. Don't be discouraged, for I am your God. I will strengthen you and help you. I will hold you up with my victorious right hand.   ISAIAH 41:10

Each time he said, "My grace is all you need. My power works best in weakness." So now I am glad to boast about my weaknesses, so that the power of Christ can work through me.   2 CORINTHIANS 12:9

Physical training is good, but training for godliness is much better, promising benefits in this life and in the life to come.   1 TIMOTHY 4:8

ℰ𝒩ot having bulging biceps or massive shoulders, a petite, slender woman might appear, at first glance, to be physically weak. Then you discover that she can run a marathon in under three hours. A bodybuilder might appear to have great strength until he demonstrates a weakness for drugs or alcohol. The Bible speaks about this tendency of strength and weakness to impersonate each other in our lives. Sometimes what seems strong is actually weak, and what appears weak is quite strong beneath the surface. External appearances are not a good indicator of internal spiritual strength. As you mature in your relationship with God, you learn to recognize your weaknesses and your strengths. Everybody has both; you cannot mature until you admit this. Thus, the presence of weakness in you need not trouble you. In fact, it is when God works through your weaknesses that he calls out the best in you. He works through your weaknesses in order to show his strength. And the best way to maximize your strengths is to exercise them by serving and helping others; then your strengths multiply through them. Using your strengths only to benefit yourself weakens you, because you become self-centered. The truly strong rely on God to use both their strengths and their weaknesses to serve and glorify him.

DIVINE PROMISE

ALL GLORY TO GOD, WHO IS ABLE, THROUGH HIS MIGHTY POWER AT WORK WITHIN US, TO ACCOMPLISH INFINITELY MORE THAN WE MIGHT ASK OR THINK. *Ephesians 3:20*

Success

MY QUESTION *for* GOD

Is it okay to try to be successful in this life?

A MOMENT *with* GOD

Work hard and become a leader; be lazy and become
a slave.   PROVERBS 12:24

Do you see any truly competent workers? They will
serve kings rather than working for ordinary people.
                                                  PROVERBS 22:29

Work willingly at whatever you do, as though you
were working for the Lord rather than for people.
                                                  COLOSSIANS 3:23

*M*any godly character traits—such as hard work,
integrity, commitment, service, and planning—often
bring material success when you apply them.

The LORD was with Joseph, so he succeeded in
everything he did as he served in the home of his
Egyptian master. Potiphar noticed this and realized
that the LORD was with Joseph, giving him success in
everything he did.   GENESIS 39:2-3

The LORD blessed Job in the second half of his life
even more than in the beginning. For now he had
14,000 sheep, 6,000 camels, 1,000 teams of oxen,
and 1,000 female donkeys.   JOB 42:12

The Scriptures contain frequent references to God's material blessings for his people. God allows his people to sometimes enjoy material blessings, but he urges them never to forget the One who gave them. It is always a bad investment to sacrifice spiritual prosperity for the sake of gaining worldly wealth.

The LORD said to Samuel, "Don't judge by his appearance or height, for I have rejected him. The LORD doesn't see things the way you see them. People judge by outward appearance, but the LORD looks at the heart."   1 SAMUEL 16:7

God's standards differ greatly from our own. He measures success not by prestige, possessions, or power, but by our motives, devotion, and commitment to him.

DIVINE PROMISE

WITH GOD'S HELP WE WILL DO
MIGHTY THINGS.   *Psalm 60:12*

Suffering

MY QUESTION *for* GOD

How can I explain suffering to someone experiencing it?

A MOMENT *with* GOD

Going over to him, the Samaritan soothed his wounds
with olive oil and wine and bandaged them. Then he
put the man on his own donkey and took him to an
inn, where he took care of him.   LUKE 10:34

Be happy with those who are happy, and weep with
those who weep.   ROMANS 12:15

If one part suffers, all the parts suffer with it, and if
one part is honored, all the parts are glad.

                                    1 CORINTHIANS 12:26

Share each other's burdens, and in this way obey the
law of Christ.   GALATIANS 6:2

Suffering is a universal experience. Some suffering
comes simply as a result of living in a fallen world, like
a car accident that maims or an illness that ravages a
loved one or even takes his or her life. Some suffering
happens by neglect, such as when we fail to prepare
for times of pressure. Sometimes we suffer by design,
when we willingly take on enormous responsibilities in
order to achieve a goal. Other times it is the result of
sin, when we stubbornly go against God's commands
and then suffer the consequences.

    Whatever the source, we all feel the dark shadow
of suffering, and we don't know how to explain it. But
we don't have to explain it. The reality is that we don't
usually know why suffering has struck us or someone
else, and one of the worst mistakes we can make is to try
to explain it out of ignorance. But everyone knows two

things about suffering: It hurts, and it helps when others bring comfort. When you join in others' suffering, you are choosing to be wounded with them, and that brings comfort. If you know someone who is hurting, walk alongside the one who is suffering, and help to bring that person—and you—comfort and hope.

DIVINE PROMISE

ALL PRAISE TO GOD, THE FATHER OF OUR LORD JESUS CHRIST. GOD IS OUR MERCIFUL FATHER AND THE SOURCE OF ALL COMFORT. HE COMFORTS US IN ALL OUR TROUBLES SO THAT WE CAN COMFORT OTHERS. WHEN THEY ARE TROUBLED, WE WILL BE ABLE TO GIVE THEM THE SAME COMFORT GOD HAS GIVEN US.

2 Corinthians 1:3-4

Surprise

MY QUESTION *for* GOD

How is God surprising?

A MOMENT *with* GOD

He has brought down princes from their thrones and exalted the humble.   LUKE 1:52

[The disciples] were shocked to find [Jesus] talking to a woman. . . . The woman left her water jar beside the well and ran back to the village, telling everyone, "Come and see a man who told me everything I ever did! Could he possibly be the Messiah?"   JOHN 4:27-29

[Jesus] gave up his divine privileges; he took the humble position of a slave and was born as a human being. When he appeared in human form, he humbled himself in obedience to God and died a criminal's death on a cross. Therefore, God elevated him to the place of highest honor and gave him the name above all other names.   PHILIPPIANS 2:7-9

God often does the opposite of what you would expect. He chose David, the youngest son of Jesse, rather than the oldest, to be king of Israel. He used a donkey to correct the pagan prophet Balaam. He took Saul, the most vicious opponent of the early church, and transformed him into Paul, the greatest and most courageous missionary of all time. He cared for and respected women in a time when they had no rights. And God used a crucifixion, the place of ultimate defeat, and made it the sign of victory over sin and death for all eternity. God's creativity and ingenuity know no boundaries. Don't limit God to the horizon of your own understanding and expectations. He wants to surprise you in ways that inspire your awe, love, gratitude, and joy. When something really good happens to you, do you feel lucky? Instead, recognize your good fortune as a divine moment from the hand of God. When you believe he is acting on your behalf, your relationship with him will grow to a deeper level.

DIVINE PROMISE

COME AND SEE WHAT OUR GOD HAS DONE,
WHAT AWESOME MIRACLES HE PERFORMS
FOR PEOPLE!   *Psalm 66:5*

Surrender

MY QUESTION *for* GOD

How does surrender to God actually bring true victory?

A MOMENT *with* GOD

I heard the Lord asking, "Whom should I send as a
messenger to this people? Who will go for us?" I said,
"Here I am. Send me."   ISAIAH 6:8

Calling the crowd to join his disciples, [Jesus] said,
"If any of you wants to be my follower, you must
turn from your selfish ways, take up your cross, and
follow me."   MARK 8:34

Either way, Christ's love controls us. Since we believe
that Christ died for all, we also believe that we have
all died to our old life. He died for everyone so that
those who receive his new life will no longer live for
themselves. Instead, they will live for Christ, who
died and was raised for them.   2 CORINTHIANS 5:14-15

Everything else is worthless when compared with the
infinite value of knowing Christ Jesus my Lord. For his
sake I have discarded everything else, counting it all as
garbage, so that I could gain Christ.   PHILIPPIANS 3:8

*M*any great battles in history ended with a surrender. One side realized that it was powerless against the other and to save themselves, admitted defeat and raised the white flag. In the spiritual realm, you fight two great battles, and surrender plays a part in both. On the one hand, you fight against sin and its control in your life. If you are not allied with God, you will surrender to sin and its deadly consequences. On the other hand, you can foolishly fight against God and his will for you because you want to have control over your life. This is a time when surrender is necessary and positive. Surrender to God comes when you finally realize that you are powerless to defeat sin by yourself and you give control of your life to God. When you are in alliance with God and the Holy Spirit lives in you, you are able to be victorious in your battle to defeat sin and experience the greatest freedom possible. When you surrender to God, you give up what you think is best for your life and do what he knows is best. You put aside your self-fulfilling ambitions so that you can do the job God has for you. You ask God to live in you and through you through the power of the Holy Spirit. You give up your attempt to control your life to God, who created you, loves you, knows you, and has a plan for you. Then you begin to experience real freedom.

DIVINE PROMISE
MY OLD SELF HAS BEEN CRUCIFIED WITH CHRIST. IT IS NO LONGER I WHO LIVE, BUT CHRIST LIVES IN ME. SO I LIVE IN THIS EARTHLY BODY BY TRUSTING IN THE SON OF GOD, WHO LOVED ME AND GAVE HIMSELF FOR ME. *Galatians 2:20*

Temptation

MY QUESTION for GOD

How does knowing my weaknesses make me strong against temptation?

A MOMENT with GOD

The LORD was with Joseph, so he succeeded in everything he did as he served in the home of his Egyptian master. Potiphar noticed this and realized that the LORD was with Joseph, giving him success in everything he did. This pleased Potiphar, so he soon made Joseph his personal attendant. He put him in charge of his entire household and everything he owned. . . . Joseph was a very handsome and well-built young man, and Potiphar's wife soon began to look at him lustfully. "Come and sleep with me," she demanded. But Joseph refused. "Look," he told her, "my master trusts me with everything in his entire household. No one here has more authority than I do. He has held back nothing from me except you, because you are his wife. How could I do such a wicked thing? It would be a great sin against God."

GENESIS 39:2-4, 6-9

𝓘sn't it interesting that Joseph was tempted with one thing he didn't have—a relationship with a woman. His brothers had stripped him of everything when they sold him into slavery—family, possessions, status. But he had remained faithful to God and regained good living conditions and authority in Potiphar's house. Yet he must have been lonely, and that is exactly where Satan struck, with the temptation to ease that loneliness.

Joseph was able to refuse the advances of Potiphar's wife because he knew why, when, and how to say no. He had determined to live a godly life in Egypt, even though no one back home would know. The pressure you may feel from the temptation to sin can best be handled by acknowledging sin as sin and determining to stand firm in your commitment to God *before* temptation knocks on your door. Standing firm may mean avoiding areas of temptation and even physically fleeing from compromising situations. Always be aware that Satan strikes where you are weakest. That's why it's important to recognize where you are vulnerable so that you will not be ambushed by temptation. If you are watching for it and praying for the strength to resist it when it comes, then, like Joseph, you will be well prepared to say no.

DIVINE PROMISE

THE TEMPTATIONS IN YOUR LIFE ARE NO DIFFERENT FROM WHAT OTHERS EXPERIENCE. AND GOD IS FAITHFUL. HE WILL NOT ALLOW THE TEMPTATION TO BE MORE THAN YOU CAN STAND. WHEN YOU ARE TEMPTED, HE WILL SHOW YOU A WAY OUT SO THAT YOU CAN ENDURE. *1 Corinthians 10:13*

Tenderness

MY QUESTION *for* GOD

How can I feel more tenderness toward others?

A MOMENT *with* GOD

You have seen what I did to the Egyptians. You know
how I carried you on eagles' wings and brought you
to myself.   EXODUS 19:4

[God said,] "I will sprinkle clean water on you, and
you will be clean. Your filth will be washed away, and
you will no longer worship idols. And I will give you
a new heart, and I will put a new spirit in you. I will
take out your stony, stubborn heart and give you a
tender, responsive heart. And I will put my Spirit in
you so that you will follow my decrees and be careful
to obey my regulations."   EZEKIEL 36:25-27

Tenderness starts in the heart of a compassionate
God. To be "carried on eagles' wings" is an image that
communicates both the power and the tenderness of
God's care for you. Although an eagle is a terrifying
predator, it is also a tender nurturer to its offspring.
The offspring can depend on it for food, protection,
and preparation for life. Likewise, the God of the universe cares for you with tenderness and compassion.
He replaces your heart hardened and dulled by years
of sin with a soft and tender heart and plants a compassionate spirit within you. When you have the tenderhearted nature of God within you, you encounter many

divine moments when you realize the depth of God's
care for you as you care for others. As you meet their
needs, your tender heart becomes more grateful for the
many ways in which God has met your own.

DIVINE PROMISE

THE LORD IS LIKE A FATHER TO HIS CHILDREN,
TENDER AND COMPASSIONATE TO THOSE WHO
FEAR HIM.   *Psalm 103:13*

Testing

MY QUESTION *for* GOD

Does God really test the quality of my faith?

A MOMENT *with* GOD

Remember how the LORD your God led you through
the wilderness for these forty years, humbling you
and testing you to prove your character, and to find
out whether or not you would obey his commands.

DEUTERONOMY 8:2

[God said,] "Jeremiah, I have made you a tester of
metals, that you may determine the quality of my
people."   JEREMIAH 6:27

Dear brothers and sisters, when troubles come your
way, consider it an opportunity for great joy. For you
know that when your faith is tested, your endurance

has a chance to grow. So let it grow, for when your endurance is fully developed, you will be perfect and complete, needing nothing. JAMES 1:2-4

*S*tudents are tested regularly for retention and understanding of the material they are learning. Auto consumers routinely take test drives to determine the quality of a vehicle before they make a purchase. Companies invest vast sums in testing their new products to guarantee that they will perform as advertised. So also, our character and spiritual commitments are tested by the fires of hardship, persecution, or suffering.

The Bible distinguishes between temptation, which Satan uses to lead us into sin, and testing, which God uses to purify us and move us toward maturity and growth. Out of testing comes a more committed faith. And out of a more committed faith comes a wiser and more committed woman. Just as commercial products are tested to strengthen their performance, God tests your faith to strengthen its resolve so that you can accomplish all God wants you to. When you feel as if your faith is being tested, see it as a divine moment when God is moving in your life to strengthen your relationship with him and help you be a greater influence.

DIVINE ENCOURAGEMENT

THESE TRIALS WILL SHOW THAT YOUR FAITH IS GENUINE. *1 Peter 1:7*

Thankfulness

MY QUESTION for GOD

How do I develop a thankful heart?

A MOMENT with GOD

Let the peace that comes from Christ rule in your hearts. For as members of one body you are called to live in peace. And always be thankful.   COLOSSIANS 3:15

Every time I think of you, I give thanks to my God.
                                            PHILIPPIANS 1:3

Since everything God created is good, we should not reject any of it but receive it with thanks.   1 TIMOTHY 4:4

Cultivate thankfulness by giving thanks regularly—to God and to others. Set aside time every day to think about what you have to be thankful for. Make a mental list of God's blessings in your life—especially the most recent ones—and thank him for them. Don't wait to feel thankful before giving thanks. Giving thanks will lead you to feel thankful. And a thankful attitude keeps you humble and helps you live in harmony with people.

It is good to give thanks to the LORD . . . to proclaim your unfailing love in the morning, your faithfulness in the evening.   PSALM 92:1-2

God has given you far more than you will ever realize—all of it undeserved, all of it given freely because of his love for you. Thank him for this before you become ungrateful and lose out on all he has yet to offer. If a blessing is worth receiving, it is worth your thanksgiving.

Divine Promise

BE THANKFUL IN ALL CIRCUMSTANCES, FOR THIS IS GOD'S WILL FOR YOU WHO BELONG TO CHRIST JESUS.   *1 Thessalonians 5:18*

Time

My Question *for* God

How does putting God first help me to manage my time?

A Moment *with* God

[Moses] told them, "This is what the LORD commanded: Tomorrow will be a day of complete rest, a holy Sabbath day set apart for the LORD. So bake or boil as much as you want today, and set aside what is left for tomorrow."   Exodus 16:23

"Remember to observe the Sabbath day by keeping it holy. You have six days each week for your ordinary work, but the seventh day is a Sabbath day of rest dedicated to the LORD your God. . . . For in six days the LORD made the heavens, the earth, the sea, and

everything in them; but on the seventh day he rested.
That is why the LORD blessed the Sabbath day and set
it apart as holy.   EXODUS 20:8-11

*B*elieve it or not, the best way to find the time you
need is to devote more time to God. Then you will know
more clearly what he wants you to do so that you can
avoid what you should not be doing. Devoting time to
God gives you the opportunity to hear his priorities for
you and allows you to focus only on what God is asking
you to do rather than on trying to do everything.

DIVINE PROMISE

TEACH US TO REALIZE THE BREVITY OF LIFE, SO
THAT WE MAY GROW IN WISDOM.   *Psalm 90:12*

Tiredness

MY QUESTION *for* GOD

What can I do when I'm tired but have to keep going?

A MOMENT *with* GOD

I am your God. I will strengthen you and help you.
I will hold you up with my victorious right hand.

                                                     ISAIAH 41:10

The Sovereign LORD is my strength! He makes me as
surefooted as a deer, able to tread upon the heights.

                                                     HABAKKUK 3:19

Jesus said, "Come to me, all of you who are weary and carry heavy burdens, and I will give you rest."

MATTHEW 11:28

Jacob's well was there; and Jesus, tired from the long walk, sat wearily beside the well about noontime.

JOHN 4:6

Be strong in the Lord and in his mighty power.

EPHESIANS 6:10

Think of all the hostility he endured from sinful people; then you won't become weary and give up. . . . So take a new grip with your tired hands and strengthen your weak knees.   HEBREWS 12:3, 12

God made you a flesh-and-blood human being. At creation he set aside one full day of rest a week because he knew you would need it. Jesus lived in a human body, so he understands what it means to be tired. He understood the limitations of his disciples and took them away for regular breaks. Life is full and busy and must be balanced by regular attention to the health of your body and your soul. Being overly tired is dangerous because it can keep you from thinking clearly and cause you to do or say something you'll regret. But when it's impossible to get enough rest, your weariness is an opportunity to experience God's faithfulness. He will give you renewed strength when you grow weary. When you come to him in praise, he refreshes your heart. When you come to him in prayer, he refreshes your soul. When you come to him in solitude, he refreshes your body. When you come to him in need, he refreshes your mind. When you come to him with thankfulness, he refreshes your perspective. Coming to God releases your burdens and allows you to draw strength from him.

DIVINE PROMISE

HE GIVES POWER TO THE WEAK AND STRENGTH TO THE POWERLESS. EVEN YOUTHS WILL BECOME WEAK AND TIRED, AND YOUNG MEN WILL FALL IN EXHAUSTION. BUT THOSE WHO TRUST IN THE LORD WILL FIND NEW STRENGTH. THEY WILL SOAR HIGH ON WINGS LIKE EAGLES. THEY WILL RUN AND NOT GROW WEARY. THEY WILL WALK AND NOT FAINT.   *Isaiah 40:29-31*

Tithing

MY QUESTION *for* GOD

I know I should tithe but I have so many other expenses. Is tithing really necessary in God's eyes?

A MOMENT *with* GOD

Honor the LORD with your wealth and with the best part of everything you produce.   PROVERBS 3:9

Give, and you will receive. Your gift will return to you in full—pressed down, shaken together to make room for more, running over, and poured into your

lap. The amount you give will determine the amount
you get back.   LUKE 6:38

If [your gift] is giving, give generously.   ROMANS 12:8

You must each decide in your heart how much to
give. And don't give reluctantly or in response
to pressure. "For God loves a person who gives
cheerfully."   2 CORINTHIANS 9:7

 *T*ithing is not just a religious law. Tithing is both practical and symbolic. Practically, tithing is a means of
supporting the church and the work of godly people
around the world. When you give, you do so because
you believe in the church and in the work it is doing.
Symbolically, giving the first part of your earnings to
the Lord demonstrates that he is your number one priority and that you are grateful for the blessings he has
given you. When you tithe, you are not only supporting
God's work, other believers, and those in need; you
are also showing your commitment to God and honor-
ing him for his provision and faithfulness. Maintaining
a habit of regular tithing is always a divine moment
because it keeps God at the top of your priority list
and gives you a proper perspective on the rest of your
paycheck. Instead of asking, "How much of my money
do I need to give to God?" ask yourself, "How much of
God's money do I need to keep?"

DIVINE PROMISE

[THE LORD SAID,] "YOU HAVE CHEATED
ME! "BUT YOU ASK, 'WHAT DO YOU MEAN?
WHEN DID WE EVER CHEAT YOU?' "YOU HAVE
CHEATED ME OF THE TITHES AND OFFERINGS
DUE TO ME.... BRING ALL THE TITHES INTO
THE STOREHOUSE SO THERE WILL BE ENOUGH
FOOD IN MY TEMPLE. IF YOU DO," SAYS THE
LORD OF HEAVEN'S ARMIES, "I WILL OPEN THE
WINDOWS OF HEAVEN FOR YOU. I WILL POUR
OUT A BLESSING SO GREAT YOU WON'T HAVE
ENOUGH ROOM TO TAKE IT IN! TRY IT! PUT ME
TO THE TEST!"   *Malachi 3:8, 10*

Unity

MY QUESTION *for* GOD

Is real unity with others possible?

A MOMENT *with* GOD

The body has many different parts, not just one part.

1 CORINTHIANS 12:14

Make every effort to keep yourselves united in the
Spirit, binding yourselves together with peace.

EPHESIANS 4:3

One of the keys to unity is to celebrate each other's
differences. Unity is not about everyone agreeing or
having the same opinion. It's about learning how to
take different opinions and direct them all toward a

shared purpose and goal. God creates everyone differently, so we should not be surprised by differences of opinion. But God also tells us to be united, which means that our differences must serve some important goal, that of bringing about the most thoughtful, well-developed plans.

Unity usually becomes difficult to achieve when we're already convinced that our opinion is the best and therefore someone else's opinion is not well thought through. This mind-set keeps us from listening to new ideas that might actually inform our own opinion for the better. We risk missing out on a potential divine moment in which God helps us see how different colors create a richer painting. Try celebrating and truly anticipating each others' differences and fitting them together to accomplish an objective. Then you will experience the true unity God designed humans to share and enjoy.

Divine Promise

YOU ARE ALL CHILDREN OF GOD THROUGH
FAITH IN CHRIST JESUS. AND ALL WHO HAVE
BEEN UNITED WITH CHRIST IN BAPTISM
HAVE PUT ON CHRIST, LIKE PUTTING ON
NEW CLOTHES. THERE IS NO LONGER JEW OR
GENTILE, SLAVE OR FREE, MALE AND FEMALE.
FOR YOU ARE ALL ONE IN CHRIST JESUS.

Galatians 3:26-28

Values

What is the power of having godly values?

A MOMENT *with* GOD

These were [Jehoshaphat's] instructions to them: "You must always act in the fear of the LORD, with faithfulness and an undivided heart."   2 CHRONICLES 19:9

No one can serve two masters. For you will hate one and love the other; you will be devoted to one and despise the other. You cannot serve both God and money.   MATTHEW 6:24

Wherever your treasure is, there the desires of your heart will also be.   LUKE 12:34

How do you spend most of your free time? Who is your favorite entertainer? Who are your best friends? What do you think about most? How do you spend your money? Your answers to these questions will show what you value most. Whatever you consider important, useful, and worth a lot is what you value. You may have heard someone described as having no values. But everyone has values, good or bad. The problem comes when you don't value what is best for you and instead let the world's values shape you. Your values are crystal clear to those around you, because what you do, where you spend your time and money, and what you talk about shows exactly what you value the most.

When you value God the most, it will be reflected in the words you speak and in how you spend your time, energy, and money. When you love and worship the Lord, obey him wholeheartedly, make godly choices, and serve others, you are displaying godly values, and your life will be purposeful in a powerful way.

DIVINE PROMISE

WHO MAY WORSHIP IN YOUR SANCTUARY, LORD? WHO MAY ENTER YOUR PRESENCE ON YOUR HOLY HILL? THOSE WHO LEAD BLAMELESS LIVES AND DO WHAT IS RIGHT, SPEAKING THE TRUTH FROM SINCERE HEARTS. *Psalm 15:1-2*

Victory

MY QUESTION *for* GOD

How do I experience victory in my life?

A MOMENT *with* GOD

King Sihon declared war on us and mobilized his forces at Jahaz. But the LORD our God handed him over to us. . . . The LORD our God also helped us conquer Aroer . . . and the whole area as far as Gilead. . . . Next we turned and headed for the land of Bashan, where King Og and his entire army attacked us at Edrei. But the LORD told me, "Do not be afraid of him, for I have given you victory over Og and his entire army." DEUTERONOMY 2:32-33, 36; 3:1-2

*W*ith God's help, the Israelites experienced victory after victory as they marched toward the Promised Land. Our greatest victory, which has been won by Christ, is receiving God's gift of salvation (see 1 John 5:4). But daily we need victory over the strongholds of sin that threaten our ability to live effectively for God and be a victorious example to others. To experience victory in the Christian life, we must be willing to commit ourselves to vigorous spiritual training and preparation (see Ephesians 6:10-18). This starts with constant prayer and consistently reading God's Word and obeying it. In these verses we see that when God was actively invited to be part of the people's lives, and when the people consistently tried to obey God's Word, they experienced victory. Too often we get so busy that we neglect spending time with God. He is no longer top priority. When we put God first, through prayer and the study of his Word, we will experience victory over our fears, and over Satan's tactics that seek to derail our relationship with God and with those we love.

DIVINE PROMISE

STUDY THIS BOOK OF INSTRUCTION
CONTINUALLY. MEDITATE ON IT DAY AND
NIGHT SO YOU WILL BE SURE TO OBEY
EVERYTHING WRITTEN IN IT. ONLY THEN WILL
YOU PROSPER AND SUCCEED IN ALL YOU DO.

Joshua 1:8

Vulnerability

MY QUESTION *for* GOD

Can I trust God with my deepest secrets?

A MOMENT *with* GOD

Search me, O God, and know my heart; test me and know my anxious thoughts. Point out anything in me that offends you, and lead me along the path of everlasting life.   PSALM 139:23-24

The word of God is alive and powerful. It is sharper than the sharpest two-edged sword, cutting between soul and spirit, between joint and marrow. It exposes our innermost thoughts and desires. Nothing in all creation is hidden from God. Everything is naked and exposed before his eyes, and he is the one to whom we are accountable.   HEBREWS 4:12-13

Confess your sins to each other and pray for each other.   JAMES 5:16

If we confess our sins to him, he is faithful and just to forgive us our sins and to cleanse us from all wickedness.   1 JOHN 1:9

What if others knew who you really are? Does this thought frighten you, or would you be okay with that? Is there anyone to whom you can or should reveal your real self: your deepest fears, hurts, sins, or doubts? Every human being has a need for that kind of intimacy, but you must choose carefully to whom you reveal your

heart. True vulnerability occurs in only the most intimate relationships because it requires that you reveal
the dark things you might have hoped would never
come out in the open. You may often resist being vulnerable with God about your sins, especially the ones
you don't want to give up, but vulnerability requires
full disclosure, not hiding or covering up. It is only
through being vulnerable that you find true healing,
restoration, renewal, and forgiveness. When you admit your sin, seek forgiveness, and commit yourself
to taking the high road, your relationship with God
and others is restored to an even higher position, and
a great weight is lifted from you. The more vulnerable
you are with God, the more his divine forgiveness frees
you from the burdens of your sin and releases you from
a life of regret and guilt. You have nothing to fear and
nothing to hide because God has changed you.

DIVINE PROMISE

THERE IS NO CONDEMNATION FOR THOSE
WHO BELONG TO CHRIST JESUS. AND BECAUSE
YOU BELONG TO HIM, THE POWER OF THE
LIFE-GIVING SPIRIT HAS FREED YOU FROM THE
POWER OF SIN THAT LEADS TO DEATH.

Romans 8:1-2

Waiting

How can waiting make my faith stronger?

A MOMENT *with* GOD

The LORD your God will drive those nations out ahead of you little by little. You will not clear them away all at once, otherwise the wild animals would multiply too quickly for you.　　DEUTERONOMY 7:22

[Jesus said,] "There is so much more I want to tell you, but you can't bear it now."　　JOHN 16:12

When the right time came, God sent his Son.

GALATIANS 4:4

*G*od often asks you to wait while he leads you along the path of progressive, not immediate, victory. Why? Sometimes this waiting keeps you from the pride that often comes after success. Sometimes it saves you from defeat. And sometimes God makes you wait to prepare you for a special task he has for you. Waiting time is never time wasted for God, so don't waste it by being anxious. Serve God as you wait for him to accomplish the next good thing in your life.

DIVINE PROMISE

BE STILL IN THE PRESENCE OF THE LORD, AND WAIT PATIENTLY FOR HIM TO ACT. *Psalm 37:7*

Will of God

How do I discover God's will for my life?

How can a young person stay pure? By obeying
your word.   PSALM 119:9

Your word is a lamp to guide my feet and a light for
my path.   PSALM 119:105

God is working in you, giving you the desire and the
power to do what pleases him.   PHILIPPIANS 2:13

God's will is for you to be holy, so stay away from all
sexual sin.   1 THESSALONIANS 4:3

"What is God's will for my life?" If you believe in God,
you have probably asked this question many times. Sometimes "God's will" seems so vague, so hard to know.
Why can't God give a divine sign that says "This Way"?
The truth is that God has already given you a whole set
of directions that will keep you in his will. He has given
you a revelation of his general will for all believers in his
written Word. The Bible has dozens of clear commands
for you to follow: Worship God only; love your neighbors and your enemies; use your spiritual gifts; tell the
truth; do not covet; do not steal; be sexually pure; remain faithful; teach your children spiritual truths; don't
gossip; be generous; don't use God's name disrespect-
fully; read his Word regularly; don't let money control

you; let the Holy Spirit control your life—and the list goes on. Isn't that God's will for your life?

In addition to God's general will, he also created each person for a specific purpose, and he calls you to do certain specific tasks. But it is usually through steady obedience to his general will that you find the specific direction for your life. In the end, when you are ushered into eternity, will it really matter what house, what car, or maybe even what job you had? The real issue will be whether you have been faithful in loving and serving God. He is vitally interested in the details of your life, but his clear will for all people is simple obedience.

DIVINE PROMISE

SEEK HIS WILL IN ALL YOU DO, AND HE WILL
SHOW YOU WHICH PATH TO TAKE.   *Proverbs 3:6*

Wisdom

MY QUESTION *for* GOD

Can I learn to be wise?

A MOMENT *with* GOD

The fear of the Lord is true wisdom; to forsake evil is real understanding.   JOB 28:28

Fear of the LORD is the foundation of true wisdom. All who obey his commandments will grow in wisdom.

PSALM 111:10

Fear of the LORD is the foundation of wisdom. Knowledge of the Holy One results in good judgment.

PROVERBS 9:10

Let the message about Christ, in all its richness, fill your lives. Teach and counsel each other with all the wisdom he gives.   COLOSSIANS 3:16

Solving a complex mathematical equation or writing a computer program requires great intelligence. But such intelligence does not guarantee a fulfilled, balanced, or productive life. Success in relationships, fulfillment of your life's purpose, and spiritual maturity are more dependent on wisdom than on intellect. Successfully navigating through life requires great wisdom, and wisdom grows out of a knowledge of God and a respect for his commands. Wisdom is what transforms head knowledge into discernment and common-sense action. True wisdom comes from God. God reveals his wisdom through his Word, but only those with humble and teachable hearts that are committed to steady obedience will absorb it. Even raw life experience doesn't always produce wisdom. Only experience prayerfully linked to the truths of Scripture allows wisdom to flourish in your life. In essence, wisdom is more about the God you know than about the facts you know.

DIVINE PROMISE

I WILL BLESS THE LORD WHO GUIDES ME; EVEN
AT NIGHT MY HEART INSTRUCTS ME.   *Psalm 16:7*

Witnessing

MY QUESTION *for* GOD

*How does God transform my testimony into the greatest story
I'll ever tell?*

A MOMENT *with* GOD

Moses told his father-in-law everything the LORD had
done to Pharaoh and Egypt on behalf of Israel.

EXODUS 18:8-11

Has the LORD redeemed you? Then speak out! Tell
others he has redeemed you from your enemies.

PSALM 107:2

[Jesus] told them, "Go into all the world and preach
the Good News to everyone."   MARK 16:15

How beautiful are the feet of messengers who bring
good news!   ROMANS 10:15

God has not given us a spirit of fear and timidity,
but of power, love, and self-discipline. So never be
ashamed to tell others about our Lord.   2 TIMOTHY 1:7-8

A friend casually mentions that she enjoyed a terrific
meal at a new restaurant and thinks you would like it
too. A stranger overhears you and your spouse discuss-
ing whether or not a certain movie would be good to
rent for a family night and offers that his kids thought
it was great. Both the friend and the stranger are witnesses. Although the word *witness* brings to mind im-
ages of courtrooms or awkward religious proselytizing,
to witness simply means to tell about something you
have experienced. All who believe in God share the
privilege and responsibility of being witnesses. Believing in God isn't about "getting in" to some exclusive
group. It's about experiencing something so wonderful
that you can't wait to invite others to experience it too.
Witnessing is really the practice of sharing your divine
moments with others. Always be ready to tell the story
of how you met and grew to love Jesus. That story is
the greatest story you can tell. Who knows? Perhaps
sharing your own story will be the pathway to a divine
moment in another's life.

DIVINE PROMISE

THOSE WHO ARE WISE WILL SHINE AS BRIGHT
AS THE SKY, AND THOSE WHO LEAD MANY
TO RIGHTEOUSNESS WILL SHINE LIKE THE
STARS FOREVER.   *Daniel 12:3*

Women

MY QUESTION *for* GOD

*What can I learn about the women who served Jesus in
his day?*

A MOMENT *with* GOD

Jesus began a tour of the nearby towns and villages,
preaching and announcing the Good News about
the Kingdom of God. He took his twelve disciples
with him, along with some women who had been
cured of evil spirits and diseases. Among them were
Mary Magdalene, from whom he had cast out seven
demons; Joanna, the wife of Chuza, Herod's business
manager; Susanna; and many others who were
contributing their own resources to support Jesus
and his disciples.   LUKE 8:1-3

In first-century Jewish culture, women were treated
as second-class citizens. They were not permitted an
education or to take part in public worship. In fact,
the Pharisees went out of their way to avoid any con-
tact with women outside their own families. The Bible
is careful to emphasize that Jesus ministered to women
in all levels of society, as seen from the list of women in
the book of Luke. The mention of Joanna as the wife of
King Herod's business manager reminds us that Jesus'
influence reached far and wide, high and low. This Bible
passage also shows the women's practical contribution
in supporting Jesus and the disciples. When the other
disciples deserted Jesus, the women continued to honor

him, remain with him, and minister to him. Jesus valued women in every way and opened the doors to their education, fellowship, and service. It seems Jesus had special insight into women's hearts and their fierce loyalty and ability to serve and worship God in unique and practical ways. When you wonder whether being a woman ever excludes you from playing a major role in God's plan, remember these women, and think again!

DIVINE PROMISE

IN THOSE DAYS I WILL POUR OUT MY SPIRIT EVEN ON SERVANTS—MEN AND WOMEN ALIKE.
Joel 2:29

Words

MY QUESTION *for* GOD

How powerful are the words I speak?

A MOMENT *with* GOD

The words of the godly are a life-giving fountain.

PROVERBS 10:11

The words of the godly are like sterling silver.

PROVERBS 10:20

Let everything you say be good and helpful, so that your words will be an encouragement to those who hear them.

EPHESIANS 4:29

*Y*our words are gifts that you give to God and to others. The things you say and the meaning behind them have enormous impact on those who hear. You wouldn't give an obscene gift to the president—or even to a friend—and it would certainly be a bad idea to give an insulting gift to an enemy. Your words are no different. In fact, the greatest gift you will ever give others is not in a box covered with paper and bows but in the words you use to encourage, inspire, comfort, and challenge them. Don't let your words be annoying, complaining, insulting, demeaning, or simply useless. Make your words count so that they can become divine moments in the lives of others.

DIVINE PROMISE

WISE WORDS ARE MORE VALUABLE THAN
MUCH GOLD AND MANY RUBIES.   *Proverbs 20:15*

Work

MY QUESTION *for* GOD

How can I glorify God as a working mom or as a stay-at-home mom?

A MOMENT *with* GOD

On the seventh day God had finished his work of creation, so he rested from all his work. . . . The LORD God placed the man in the Garden of Eden to tend and watch over it.   GENESIS 2:2, 15

*W*hether you work outside the home or at home raising your children, your work is anchored in God's character; part of being made in his image is sharing the industrious and creative aspects of his nature. Your abilities to show creativity and responsibility at work and at home will inspire those same qualities in your family as they see your efforts to support them and to glorify God.

Whether you eat or drink, or whatever you do, do it all for the glory of God.   1 CORINTHIANS 10:31

*W*hatever job God has called you to do, you do it with excellence and commitment because you serve a God of excellence and commitment. In whatever situation God has placed you, you have an opportunity to demonstrate a divine standard of excellence and commitment to those around you.

Some people work wisely with knowledge and skill, then must leave the fruit of their efforts to someone who hasn't worked for it. This, too, is meaningless, a great tragedy.   ECCLESIASTES 2:21

Never be lazy, but work hard and serve the Lord enthusiastically.   ROMANS 12:11

Work willingly at whatever you do, as though you were working for the Lord rather than for people. Remember that the Lord will give you an inheritance as your reward.   COLOSSIANS 3:23-24

God wants you to work diligently and with enthusiasm at whatever you do, whether you're out showing houses or at home raising your children. When you think of your daily tasks as having been assigned by God, you will find yourself working for his approval rather than for others' approval. When you work enthusiastically for God, you can be proud of the work you do, whether your workplace is at home or in some other place.

DIVINE PROMISE

GOD IS NOT UNJUST. HE WILL NOT FORGET HOW HARD YOU HAVE WORKED FOR HIM AND HOW YOU HAVE SHOWN YOUR LOVE TO HIM BY CARING FOR OTHER BELIEVERS. *Hebrews 6:10*

Worry

MY QUESTION *for* GOD

What can help when worry overwhelms me?

A MOMENT *with* GOD

Don't worry about tomorrow, for tomorrow will bring its own worries. Today's trouble is enough for today. MATTHEW 6:34

[Jesus said,] "Here on earth you will have many trials and sorrows. But take heart, because I have overcome the world." JOHN 16:33

*W*orry is a misuse of your God-given imagination. Most of the things you worry about never even happen, so when you worry, you may be wasting your time and emotional energy for nothing. When you feel consumed by worry, make a conscious effort to turn those thoughts into prayer. Tell God your concerns, and turn them over to him to handle. There is no problem that he cannot overcome. If almighty God is taking care of you, you have no need to worry.

DIVINE PROMISE

THE LORD KEEPS WATCH OVER YOU AS YOU COME AND GO, BOTH NOW AND FOREVER.
Psalm 121:8

Worship

MY QUESTION *for* GOD

Why is worshiping God important?

A MOMENT *with* GOD

They know the truth about God because he has made it obvious to them. For ever since the world was created, people have seen the earth and sky. Through everything God made, they can clearly see his invisible qualities—his eternal power and divine nature.   ROMANS 1:19-20

*Y*ou have an instinct for worship. All human beings were created to worship. To worship is to ascribe ultimate value to an object or person and then to revere, adore, pay homage to, and obey by ordering the priorities of your life around the object of your worship. The Bible teaches that God alone is worthy of your worship. Worship, more than anything else, will connect you with God.

God is Spirit, so those who worship him must worship in spirit and in truth. JOHN 4:24

*G*od wants us to gather with other believers for regular times of worship. But worship is not confined to formal places and times. What is required is that you worship God with your whole spirit and in truth according to God's true person and nature. You can do that anytime and anywhere. When you learn to worship at any time or place, you will find yourself experiencing God's presence throughout your day.

Oh, how great are God's riches and wisdom and knowledge! How impossible it is for us to understand his decisions and his ways! For who can know the LORD's thoughts? Who knows enough to give him advice? And who has given him so much that he needs to pay it back? For everything comes from him and exists by his power and is intended for his glory. All glory to him forever! Amen. ROMANS 11:33-36

Take time to praise God whenever you see his wisdom, power, direction, care, and love in your life. When you do, worship becomes a way of life that deepens your relationship with God and strengthens your ability to communicate with him.

DIVINE PROMISE

COME, LET US WORSHIP AND BOW DOWN.
LET US KNEEL BEFORE THE LORD OUR MAKER,
FOR HE IS OUR GOD. WE ARE THE PEOPLE HE
WATCHES OVER, THE FLOCK UNDER HIS CARE.
Psalm 95:6-7

Worth

MY QUESTION *for* GOD

How am I worthy to be a follower of God?

A MOMENT *with* GOD

[Jesus said,] "I have given you authority over all the power of the enemy, and you can walk among snakes and scorpions and crush them. Nothing will injure you. But don't rejoice because evil spirits obey you; rejoice because your names are registered in heaven."

LUKE 10:19-20

There is no condemnation for those who belong to Christ Jesus. And because you belong to him, the power of the life-giving Spirit has freed you from the power of sin that leads to death. The law of Moses was unable to save us because of the weakness of our sinful nature. So God did what the law could not do. He sent his own Son in a body like the bodies we sinners have. And in that body God declared an end to sin's control over us by giving his Son as a sacrifice for our sins. ROMANS 8:1-3

Don't think you are better than you really are. Be honest in your evaluation of yourselves, measuring yourselves by the faith God has given us. ROMANS 12:3

Most of us struggle to see ourselves with twenty-twenty vision! Either we fail to see our faults, or we fail to see our value. God loves you for who you are, not because of what you do for him. God loved you before you made your first mistake, before you uttered your first word, and even before you took your first breath. His love for you is an eternal thread woven throughout your life and fortified through the life, death, and resurrection of Jesus on your behalf. It is hard to believe that God's approval doesn't depend on what you do. Sometimes it is easy to get so caught up in the experience of serving God that you lose sight of the greatest privilege of all—knowing God and being known by him. To have your name registered as a citizen of heaven means that you belong, without question, to the eternal kingdom of God. Nothing else you do on earth can compare with that privilege or joy. Don't get caught in the trap of basing your identity or self-worth on your performance. Rejoice that they are based on God's unconditional love.

DIVINE PROMISE

YOU MADE [PEOPLE] ONLY A LITTLE LOWER THAN GOD AND CROWNED THEM WITH GLORY AND HONOR.   *Psalm 8:5*

Index

DIVINE MOMENTS
Books

DIVINE MOMENTS for WOMEN
Everyday Inspiration from God's Word

DIVINE MOMENTS
Everyday Inspiration from God's Word

DIVINE MOMENTS for MEN
Everyday Inspiration from God's Word

DIVINE MOMENTS for STUDENTS
Everyday Inspiration from God's Word

DIVINE MOMENTS for LEADERS
Everyday Inspiration from God's Word

FEATURING THE New Living Translation

FEATURING THE New Living Translation